World War II

and Me

and

the

Phantom Battalion

20 Wilbur Brooker

Lei Footner

World War II
and Me

and

the

Phantom Battalion

Lee Fortner

To order additional copies of this book, contact:
Xlibris Corporation
1-888-795-4274
www.Xlibris.com
Orders@Xlibris.com
39378

Contents

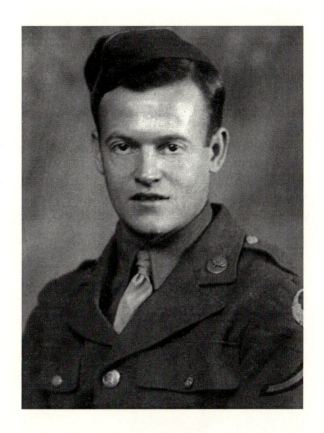

Dedicated to:
My brother . . . Ken (1917-1980)
8th U.S. Air Force

"Hey, buddy, pass the salt!"

ACKNOWLEDGEMENTS

I AM INDEBTED to my *good friend* and *fellow soldier* Tom *Buschmohle* for providing our *battlefield map*.

INTRODUCTION

THE 186TH FIELD Artillery Battalion was one of the *'fightingest,'* most *'crack' artillery* outfits of World War II, which its record of **181** *consecutive days of firing* aggressive and evasive action towards the enemy certainly attests. It supported and fought alongside practically every infantry division, and many armored and tank divisions, of the 1st U.S. Army, and the British 7th Armored Division, which is why I call it the **Phantom Battalion**. This name is my own; you will not find it documented anywhere else.

I am proud to have fought with the good men of the 186th Field Artillery of the United States Army in World War II. The 186th fought in 5 major battle campaigns across *Europe: Normandy, Northern France, Central Europe, Rhineland, and Ardennes*, venturing from the western shores of France to eastern Czechoslovakia. We fought in over 20 major battles, including Omaha beach, St. Lo, and the Battle of the Bulge.

I have always felt very lucky to have survived and been able to return home, free of any major injury, to live my life as a civilian, because so many others did not.

These are some of the stories I remember as the major events of my experience of the war, both personally, and in battle. I have tried to combine *personal stories*, some *humorous* and some *serious*, with *basic Battalion battle diary*. I hope that this makes for an *interesting mix* of reading to tell the story of my war experience.

This book is, *actually*, dedicated to *all of those who took part* in the Allied war effort and helped to defeat Hitler and the Nazis, and their allies, and save the world from Nazi and fascist domination, but especially to *all of the military men who lost their lives* in battle in that effort. The *true heroes* of this war *gave their lives* so that others could remain living *free*. God Bless them all.

Needless to say, Bless all of the poor souls who lost their lives to Nazi atrocities, and all of the civilians killed in the war. These were the true victims.

1

The Notice

THE MOST *UN-WELCOME* letter ever written was *undoubtedly* the one I received in January of 1943. The wording is not *exact*, but it went something like:

> *'Greetings, you have been selected to represent and serve your country . . . etc. . . . . etc. . . . etc. . . . therefore, you are ordered to report to your draft board on the following date.'*
> *. . . signed . . . The President of the United States*

Up to this time, I was keeping my fingers crossed that I would be deferred. My mother was 63 years old, and I was the only one left at home. Brother Ken was drafted a month or so earlier. I was working at a defense plant, Quincy Barge Builders, thinking and hoping this would help keep me at home. It so happened that only *skilled* workers were deferred. I was a chauffeur and mail clerk. Sorry!

I reported to the draft board for registration and a physical. About two weeks later, I boarded a bus along with some 20 other guys. As if it was a secret, they didn't even say where we were headed. About 2 hours down the road we saw a sign: 'Scott Air Force Base – this way.'

My first thought, *"Boy, I'm going to be in the Air Force, maybe even with my brother!"* No such luck! We were there just long enough for another physical *(one is not enough!)* and an IQ test.

All of the *dummies* were sent to Ft. Sill, Oklahoma!

2

Life in Ft. Sill, Oklahoma

BEING FROM ILLINOIS, I thought I was pretty well adjusted to the winter weather, but upon arriving in Oklahoma in the winter of 1943, I soon put that notion out of my head! We arrived during the night, on a *vintage* type train. It was *'cold as hell!'* . . . Agitated by a brisk north wind. My first impression of Oklahoma was, *"You can have it!"*

We were assigned to some barracks that I swear must have been built during the days of the Indian wars! *Single-board construction!* . . . You could actually see through the walls! One un-lit, wood-burning stove stood in the middle of the room. Thank God we only stayed there for one night! The next day we moved into permanent housing, barracks in Ft. Sill proper.

Basic training in those days was for 13 weeks. I stayed on for an extra 6 or 7 weeks as an *assistant calisthenics instructor.* This I didn't mind; I sort-of liked it, especially when they gave me that *arm-band* with *'acting corporal stripes.'* Now I was *somebody!* *Ha-ha*! (The only down-fall being that when someone *'goofed up'* more than once, the Sergeant would say, *"Private 'so-and-so,' 'you're to do 2 laps around the field (a football-field size field)! And Corporal Fortner, you go with him to see that he gets back!"* (He got punished . . . *and so did I*!)

Basic training was difficult. Getting used to getting up at 5 am, getting dressed and in formation by 6 am, and then off to the athletic field for calisthenics, which lasted an hour. Breakfast was next, then rest for 30 minutes. Then the day began. It may be to the rifle range, or perhaps a nice little hike with full backpack (some 25 lbs). The first one being only 5 miles, working up to 10, to 15, to 20, and finally the grand finale of 25 miles! With *full backpack*! In *90 to 100 degree heat*! With a *tough* drill-sergeant! *'Make my day!'* as Clint would say!

Long Hike at Ft. Sill

There were some fun times, too. A close friend, Paul, and I used to go into town occasionally. Norman, Oklahoma was just a few miles away. We parted company when he decided to transfer to the paratroopers. He wanted me to transfer, too! *"Who, me? . . . No way!"* We used to spend some evenings in the summer time outside doing *push-up* contests. He was a good, clean-cut guy. Never did hear from him after that. I hope he made it through it all.

Occasionally, a U.S.O. troop would perform for us at the Fort. One time in particular, I remember Jinx Faulkenberg appeared with a troop of other performers, including a dance band. At the time, Big Bands were in! Jinx was a gorgeous, *'up-and-coming' movie-star.* You can imagine the place being *packed* that night! Soon the M.C. announced that Jinx *would dance with everyone*! All you had to do was form a line. As luck would have it, I had a pretty good spot in the line. One after one, she danced about 5 seconds with each. Soon it was my turn. I was a little nervous, but I enjoyed my 5 seconds! I thought, *"Boy, getting to hold and dance with a movie-star like Jinx Faulkenberg! Wow!"*

My first experience as a *guard* came on Easter Sunday, 1943. They asked for volunteers from the ranks of those who hadn't planned on going to church service. I really felt important, as I got to sport a *.45 revolver* on my hip! Big time! Plus, those *acting corporal stripes* on my arm!

3

Watermelon in Chattanooga

SOME BUDDIES AND I went into Chattanooga, Tennessee one day on an *8-hour pass*. We shopped for *chigger-bite* medication and a few other personal items, before stopping in a few bars. It felt so good to sit at a bar and relax, so different than being up in the hills! Chattanooga was a nice, friendly town. Although over-run with G.I.s, they were still friendly people.

We probably had a little too much to drink, which '*back-fired*'a little later . . . '*later*'being after we spotted vendors on the street corners selling slices of ice-cold *watermelon*! M-m-m . . . good! I can remember me and my buddies walking down the street eating watermelon, spitting the seeds on the ground. *M-m-m-m . . . so good!*

Beer is good. Watermelon is good. But they weren't meant to be *mixed*! At the end of the day, we caught our army-truck ride back to the hills. After all the *bumps* in the road, with the sun shining so *brightly*, we soon felt the *ill-effects* of the combination! We were all as '*sick as dogs!*'

4

A Heel of a Time!

WE WERE ON maneuvers in Tennessee in the summer of 1943. I was assigned to be a cannoneer (one of six or eight men to maneuver the *'trails'* of the Howitzer whenever it needed to be moved into a different position.) While doing so one time, I slipped and *fell*, and the trail *fell* on the heel of my *foot*! I was lucky that it wasn't on my foot proper. It surely would have crippled it. I was sent to a near-by *field hospital*, which was in a large tent. I spent a couple of days recuperating and had a sore foot for some time. This ended my cannoneer days.

So they put me in *communications*, laying phone lines to each of the four guns in our battery. Usually, we had to do this in pitch darkness, with the aid of our flashlight, and, if lucky, by the light of the moon. We (our battalion) always traveled by night, if possible, and in reaching our new position would have to get *set-up* immediately and be ready in case of a *'fire mission'*.

We laid the wire on the ground whenever possible, but at times had to throw them over bushes, tree limbs or whatever else. After being in communications a few months, they started training me in *'fire mission control.'* (I go into this deeper in "Maneuvers in the Moors.")

I liked this aspect of my job, although it entailed a lot of responsibility. It was at this time that I was promoted to *Corporal (Tech 5th grade)* . . . *known as a T-5!* In our outfit, you got promoted only when there was an opening! In our section (*the wire section*) there were 3 of us: *a sergeant, a corporal, and a Tech 5.* The three of us took care of the wire communications for our battery for the entire length of the war.

If a line got broken, which happened quite often, one of us three would have to go trace the line, find the break, and repair it. Often this happened during a '*fire mission.*' If the line was out, the gun was out: *so it had to be fixed no matter what!* After connecting up to the gun, each man would find time to dig his own *fox-hole.* It sounds impossible to be in a *fox-hole* anywhere near a Howitzer and actually *sleep!* . . . But when you got tired enough, you slept like a baby. And you always slept with your *carbine* (rifle) right next to you!

If you like *chiggers* and *mosquitoes,* the Tennessee hills are the place to be. I'd swear, 6 mosquitoes could carry you away! Chiggers, *that's another story.* We tried every remedy known to soothe the problem: over-the-counter medication, rubbing alcohol, finger-nail polish. Nothing worked! We even tried *gasoline!* I never stopped itching until we got out of that *insect-ridden place!*

From there it was *home* to Quincy, Illinois, for *a **30-day furlough!*** . . . ***Whoopie!****! Bring on the girls!*

It so happened that my brother Ken came home on furlough a few days later. He was in the Air Force, stationed in Oregon. We both really enjoyed being home with Mom and all the family. I came home *un-announced, surprising Mom by knocking on the door, then stepping aside until she answered!* She almost had a *heart attack! (Sorry, Mom!)* We all really enjoyed ourselves, but all too soon, it was time for us to go. Ken had to report somewhere in Oregon, and I had to report to Ft. Dix, New Jersey.

5

Brother Ken

F ROM FT. DIX, New Jersey *(an 'embarkation' camp)*, we would be *shipped-out over-seas*. It was just a matter when, and where. During my stay there (some 6 weeks), from time to time, we had to march to the other side of camp, for one reason or another. On one of these marches, while passing a line of barracks, I noticed a guy that looked like **Ken**! *I couldn't believe it! He was supposed to be in Oregon – some 1500 miles away!* Without thinking, I started to walk out of formation over towards him! The guy in back of me grabbed me, saying, *"Hey, you can't do that!"* Quietly, I noticed the name on the street sign, and which barrack I was looking at.

Upon returning to our barracks, I hurriedly found First Sergeant Kelly, telling him the situation, and *pleading* with him to give permission for me to go find Ken! He said he couldn't do that, since everyone was to be on a *moment's notice* in case of a *ship-out* order. But being the nice guy that he was, he added that . . . *if he didn't know, then he couldn't say where I was. On that note I was out the door!*

Returning to the place where I saw him, I inquired as to where Ken might be found. Finally, someone said, *"Try the mess-hall."* (It was about meal time.) As I entered the hall, I stood and looked around, hoping to *spot* him. Soon I asked another G.I. passing by, *"Do you know Kenny Fortner of the 356ᵗʰ wing?"* Luckily, *he did!*. . . And soon spotted where he was sitting.

As I had hoped, there was room to sit *next* to him. I was getting a lot of *looks* and *finger-pointing* as they noticed I was a stranger, and resembled Kenny. I walked over and *sat down next to him.* He didn't notice me, as he was busy eating. Earlier, I had gotten in the *'chow line'* and filled my plate. I sat there as if I were one of them. All the guys around kept starring at me, wondering who I was and what I was doing there. Soon they found out, as I tapped my brother on the shoulder and said, **"Hey, buddy, pass the salt."**

As I uttered these words, Kenny's head *swung around!* His eyes seemed as big as *apples* as he *stood*-up and *grabbed* me! *"Lee!"* he said, *"I can't believe it!!"* At this moment, every *'fly-boy'* around *applauded* and *laughed!* Then we all settled down to visit and finish our meal.

From the *mess-hall,* we went to his barracks to visit, remembering our recent furlough at home and how wonderful it was to see Mom and all the family. Soon it was time for me to leave. The 1ˢᵗ Sergeant said to be back by 8 p.m. *or else!*

6

Trip to New York City

WE DECIDED TO celebrate our fortunate meeting by getting a *12-hour pass* and go into **New York City**. Buses were provided for the occasion. I took one of my buddies, and so did Ken. We hit **Times' Square**, went from bar to bar, and eventually wound up at the **Waldorf-Astoria Hotel**! . . . A *huge* place! . . . With many different bars and cafes. We ventured into this one bar-room, barely stepped inside, and quickly noticed that we were not welcome, as everyone there was dressed formally, and all eyes were upon us as we entered. On the other hand, the one we spent some time in was very hospitable: and we had an enjoyable time there.

Before leaving camp, I called home to sister Frannie, to tell her our plans for the evening, and that we would call her at 8 p.m., and to have *everyone* there so we could say '*Hello*' to all! (Fran & Les had the only telephone in the family.) *Unfortunately*, Ken was a little *inebriated* and when it was his turn to talk, he got *sick* in the phone-booth!!

Naturally, this cut our conversation *short*! I apologized and hung up, and we hurriedly left the area! All in all, we had a *great* time. We enjoyed each other's company; our friends '*hit-it-off*' well, and new friendships were made. Ken and I promised to write to each other often. We didn't know *when* we would be *shipped out* or *where to*. This could have been our last meeting.

Oh yes, about that bus trip back to camp . . . Since this was a camp of embarkation, regulations governing securing a pass demanded that you be back on time! The penalties were severe! Well, this was the bus-driver's *first* trip into New York City and back! Of course, we were all feeling good, so good, in fact, that Ken & I and our friends were standing around the driver *singing songs* and having fun! This *undoubtedly* led to what was about to happen!

Suddenly, the driver *slowed-up* and *pulled-off* to the side of the road. I said, "*What's wrong?*" He said, "*Well, you know that 'Y' in the road back there? I took the 'right' turn, but feel that was wrong.*" I looked at my watch. It was about *2 a.m.*, and we were to be back by *3 a.m. . . . or else!*

None of us knew exactly how many miles we had yet to go. I looked at the driver and said, "*If you think you are wrong, turn this thing around and get back on the right road! We have to be back on time.*" Good thing I did, probably: *all the other guys were drunk and didn't know what was happening!* Luck was with us, though. We got back in the '*nick-of-time,*' . . . with only some *5* minutes to go! (*Needless to say, when we stopped the bus back up the road, we stopped our singing, too!*)

At the Waldorf-Astoria, New York City: Ken, Me and Tom.

7

Convoy to England

SOON IT WAS time to **'ship-out.'** This required more *inoculations*, more *this*, and more *that*. Finally, we were told we were going to **Europe.** They were so *secretive* that they wouldn't say where in Europe *until we were actually at sea!* Then we were told it was **England.**

The ship I was on was named "*William & Mary*." It was an English-owned ship, and manned by English sailors, but was leased by the U.S. We spent *10 days* at sea, *10 boring* yet *wonderful* days!

After the first two days, we got suspicious as to why we were getting only *Brussel sprouts, mutton, and some greasy substitute for sausage!* This was a big ship, holding some **5,000 men**, and the Officers' quarters were on the *top deck.* Our quarters *(our immediate outfit)* were some *2 or 3 stories below deck! . . . Near the bottom of the hull!* Next to us was the *'hold' (the storage compartment).* This was where all the supplies for the voyage were stored. Someone *discovered* this compartment and *broke-open* the locks! To our surprise, they found *American food*: such as *steaks, chops, and everything else! . . . and all the good brands of cigarettes!*

At the ships commissaries, they were selling only the *cheap brands* of *cigarettes* and holding the good ones, as well as the *steaks* and other *meats,* for *'black-market'* sale back in England! These were *American* supplies, *paid for by Americans*, meant to feed *American* men at sea! We found out that the officers were getting theirs, so there would be no suspicion, *had we not discovered it!*

Anyway, many of us that night *raided* the meat locker and took the meat up to the various commissaries, where they did *short-order* type cooking. We ordered the English to cook these for us. At first they '*balked*,' but we soon changed their minds by *threatening* to throw them *over-board*! We really had a *feast* that night! The word must have gotten to the Captain of the ship, because *after that, the food at meal-time improved!*

The English cooks weren't the only ones *threatened*. One of our *own* officers was told to *stay up on top deck for the trip*, or he may get *tossed* as well! No one liked him. He was as G.I. as could be. I really think it could have happened to him. He must have thought so, too, as he never came down to visit his men!

As I said, our quarters were below deck, and this I *never liked*! For one reason, the ship, being made of *steel*, made lots of *vibrations* from the motors: and when the winds were high, they were *terrible*! Also, I had this fear of being *trapped*. There were many nights I spent *on deck*. Although this wasn't allowed, I got by with it anyway.

The days went slow, although you could roam the ship at will, except top-deck. The ship was some **5** decks high! Day or night, there were '*crap-games*' and *poker* going on everywhere, besides *reading*, and *writing letters* home. It was about the only recreation we had.

Our ship was but 1 in a convoy of probably **50**! We were told it was the largest convoy to date! This alone was reason enough for the *German subs* to attack! . . . As well as the *Luftwaffe*! It was day-time, and suddenly the *alarm* sounded! We were under **attack**! Over the 'loud-speaker' came, "***All Army personnel below deck!* . . . Immediately**!" *I was scared to death!* I didn't relish the thought of being *below-deck* while maybe being hit by a *torpedo*, so I, and a friend, took shelter beneath an army truck. (Many army vehicles were anchored-down on the decks.) The loud *strafing* of **bullets** from a German plane *ricocheting* across the metal deck, and the noise from our '*ack-ack*' guns sent *chills* down my spine. This was my first taste of action. It was *scary as hell* being at sea and feeling helpless, like a sitting target!

Suddenly, **a bomb exploded near-by!** No damage done – *except to my nerves*! Miraculously, at least to my knowledge at the time, no ships were seriously damaged. Our '*ack-ack*' *(anti-aircraft)* guns and navy destroyers chased them off. Luckily, they never attacked again. This was quite an experience!

Soon it was time to reach our destination – *Liverpool, England.* The night before, we, myself and many others, raided the '*hold*' again, this time for *cigarettes*! We actually threw everything that our duffle-bag held *out the port-holes*, and filled it with cartons of the *cigarettes* that were *meant* to be ours all the time! Later, after we landed, we were issued new supplies to replace the ones gone '*over-board.*' We simply '*lost them,*' . . . didn't know what happened to them!

I would have liked to have seen the *expressions* on the '*blimy,*' English sailors' *faces* when they discovered what happened! We really should have reported this to the '*higher-ups*' in Washington D.C.!

As we pulled into the harbor, it was after dark. I can still hear all the many fog-horns *sounding-off.* . . . *What a sound!* (It was always foggy there.) Now, it was time, again, to "*hurry-up and wait*" . . . *The old Army game.* You were always *hurrying-up* or *waiting* on *something* . . . this time, for your turn to walk off the boat. It seems to me it was very late-evening when we actually did get off of the ship.

8

Maneuvers in the Moors

THE FIRST TIME we used 'live' ammo was on maneuvers in the English Moors. It was damp and soggy, with tall grasses everywhere. We looked forward to using 'live' ammo. The 155 mm Howitzer used a **97**-pound shell, and with full *'powder-charge'* could shoot **9 and ½ miles**! Quite a deadly weapon! We were there probably a week. I considered it an endurance test as well.

After laying phone-line to the guns, I was given training in the *'command-post,'* which I used throughout the war. There we had a *'make-shift'* shelter, made of canvas and *camouflage-netting*. My job was to *relay* the *commands* to the phone operators at each *gun*, just as they came to me over the phone from *headquarters battery*. An officer was next to me, on another phone, to verify the message. *For example*: the phone would ring, and a voice would say, *"Fire Mission!! Elevation: 'so-and-so,' range: 'so-and-so,' powder charge: 'so-and-so.'"* After giving this message to the guns, they were to *report-in* as *ready*! When headquarters said, *"Fire!"* . . . *instantly, they did!*

A small, single-engine *'spotter'* plane relayed back the accuracy of the firing. I remember staying in the *"phone-booth"* for some **36** to **48** *hours at a time*, with only a **10**-*minute break*, when needed!

Something happened up on the Moors which was really funny! It seems the English hunters didn't know we were there, or didn't care, let-alone know that we were using "*live*" ammo! *Suddenly, directly ahead of us, was the sound of bugles blowing; then the sound of many hound-dogs; then the poor, little, red fox with a bunch of guys dressed in their hunting garb, red hats and all, chasing after, running right by us! Firing range or no firing range, nothing stops the fox hunt!*

9

Life in England

W E SPENT SOME *8 months* in England prior to D-Day. Our *'camp-site'* was located on the southwestern coast, maybe 5 miles from the sea, directly across from Wales. Strange as it may seem, I was never on the beach! We were kept busy all the time, and not permitted to leave the base, except on a *regulated-pass*. When I did get a pass, it was usually to go into town. Get this – the name of the town was *"Whatchit-and-Willington"*! Digest that one!

It was a small town, the one or two *'pubs'* being the main attraction, there patrons being mostly G.I.s, although some English, too. Their version of beer was *"ale-and-bitters." Uck-k-k!! (Not for me!)* . . . A *dartboard* on the wall was about the only entertainment. Occasionally, a *spirited fight* might break out!

The daily military routine was similar to basic-training: up at 5 a.m., calisthenics, then breakfast. Rifle-range was always a favorite of mine.

Several times we went to scale the cliffs. On the southern coast of England are located many cliffs. They are really huge, and straight up! I'll never forget that all of us did quite well, *except one of the Lieutenants*! He was really *embarrassed*! Everyone could *'shimmy'* up the rope, *swing* out to get momentum, and *keep going, except him*! He took it in stride, though, *laughing* about it.

Looking back, I don't know why I didn't have a *camera* to record things like this. Maybe one reason was the fact that film was *hard* to '*come-by.* My sister would send me *film* when it could be had, and I would mail the completed rolls back to her to get developed. She would mail me some photos if I requested them. *All-in-all*, I just didn't take many *photos*, which I now regret. Well, blame that on '*rationing*!'

Speaking of that, back home everything was being '*rationed*': *gasoline, coffee, sugar, even canned fruit.* Pineapple was my favorite, so my Mom would send me cans of pineapple whenever she could '*haggle*' some out of the local grocery stores where she shopped. The manager of Kroger's would "*save*" her a can whenever he could, by keeping it under the counter, with her name on it.

Whenever I received a can of pineapple from home, *I would hide it!* I slept on the *top bunk*, and I remember that, waiting until *very late at night*, I would, *very quietly*, get my can of pineapple and my little can-opener, and *very slowly, very quietly open it,* and *savor every bite!* It was customary to share your goodies from home – *but not my pineapple*!

All the guys in my outfit w*ere pretty good guys. Some were quite talented. One was a barber, one a tailor (self-made), one even a financier*! One guy would stand at the end of the line on '*pay-day*,' waiting to collect his dues from anyone who owed him money. He would loan money to anyone for any reason, but you had to '*pay*-up' on '*pay-day*.' I always thought that maybe his parents were in the '*loan-shark*' business! Of course, he charged *interest*!

We washed our clothes the '*primitive*' way. There were 2 empty *50-gallon barrels* behind each barrack. One to '*boil*' your clothes in, with G.I. soap, (*that would kill or clean anything!*), and the other to *rinse* in. First, you had to *build a fire (of wood),* and keep it going for the wash-water. We'd dry then on a line. Milt, the tailor, would '*hand-press*' your clothes for a *small fee. Believe me,* he was kept *busy*! Of course, he did this on his *own* time in the evening. He would also sew *buttons* on, and mend clothes.

Ray, the *barber,* was another *popular* guy. He, too, practiced his trade during his free-hours: *15-cents for a haircut*! Sounds cheap, but a *private's pay* was only *$21.00 per month, after life-insurance of $6.75 was deducted*! What do you think of that!? You were *drafted* into service, thus *endangering* your life, *and then were made to pay for your own life insurance!* Ten-thousand dollars coverage was the norm, for $6.75 per month, regardless of age. By the time you bought *personal items,* got a *haircut,* paid the *tailor,* had a few '*ale & bitters,*' . . . *you had better had enough left to pay-off your loan from Joe! Sounds like we needed a union!*

We had our own Chaplain, who performed services for the Protestants, the Catholics, and the Jews. He was also instrumental in contacting family members in cases of emergency.

Army life always consisted of keeping your *living-quarters clean and orderly,* with *daily inspections.* At '*roll-call*' each morning, you had better had *shiny shoes, clean clothes, and be well-groomed!* Or it meant *K.P. (kitchen patrol.)* or *guard duty! Scrubbing* the wooden floors with G.I. soap and brush, *on hands and knees,* was a weekly *ritual.* Dusting the walls and woodwork was included. Afterwards, the Captain would come in for *inspection,* with everyone standing at "**Attention**!" I always hoped that he was in a good mood. *If not,* one of his favorite antics would be to reach up high on the window ledge with his finger, claiming it was dirty. *If so,* he ordered the *whole clea*ning to be *done over*! – "**NOW**!" *He was our beloved Captain!*

In the evening hours, a lot of the guys would be practicing their skill at *poker,* or '*craps,*' or *writing letters home,* or doing their *laundry 'out back.'* There was never a dull moment! Almost a daily routine, of course, was "*drill march*ing." "Hup, two, three, four! Hup, two, three, four! . . ." *Oh, what memories!*

10

Hectic Night in London

WHENEVER KEN AND I got a chance to visit one-another, it was always enjoyable: *two brothers, over-seas in the same country – how great!* This time, we met in London. I really enjoyed the *train-ride* there, probably 100 miles. Those English trains are *something!* What made it so different from ours were the *compartments*: quite comfortable, seating 6 passengers, or so. Of course, there was a lot of G.I.s going back and forth to London. (With all of our troops over there, the population was probably *doubled!*)

Arriving at the train station, Kenny was there to meet me. He had only 30 miles to go to get there, and it was easy for him to get a *'pass'* just about *anytime!* So, he spent a lot of time in the city. On this particular day, we just *'bummed'* around, enjoying each others company. Come lunch time, we stopped at a small, quaint, little *'pub'* that served food.

We hadn't been seated long, when 2 *Russian* soldiers approached us, and, in broken English, asked if they might sit at our table, as the place was quite full. We obliged, and soon they struck-up a conversation. I could soon tell that they could have been *spies* by the *questions* they asked, and the *answers* they wanted: *as to where we were stationed and what kind of outfit we were from.* I *winked* at Ken, and we told them *nothing.*

We were always warned about giving out any military '*info*' to anyone! They offered to trade us Russian vodka for American cigarettes. We didn't take any vodka, but we gave them a pack of '*cig.s*' each, anyway! This made them happy, and soon they were on their way. The Russians were our allies at the time, but all countries have spies working, all of the time!

The English version of beer, '*ale & bitters*,' never did agree with me very much. We visited a few '*pubs*' that afternoon, which is the reason I had a *headache* a few hours later. On this trip, Kenny brought a couple of his G.I. buddies along. We all had our names registered to stay at the YMCA that evening. Upon arriving, Ken had heard of a *skating rink* on the other side of town. He and his buddies wanted to go there, and asked me to go along. Ken was always an avid skater and decided to go. Me, I was getting a *headache* from the '*ale & bitters*' and decided to stay. I told them to go on ahead.

There was bus service to the rink. Although the city of London was under air-attack every night, this did not stop much of the '*night-life*' from carrying on. My *headache* was coming on strong, and I knew that I should *lie-down* for a spell. They assigned me to a room on the third floor: *a gigantic room – more like a hall! – With floor-to-ceiling windows all on one end of the room.* I remember there was one other G.I. in bed. (*There were 20, or so, beds in the very large room.*) I believe he was *drunk*, and fell asleep!

I tried to get some sleep, but couldn't. After an hour or so, a loud burst of '**air-raid**' *sirens* rang out, then the horrifying sound of a '*buzz-bomb*' coming in! I rolled out of bed yelling at the other guy to "**Hit the floor!**" . . . which he did. The bomb hit close by, *shattering* all the large, glass windows. Neither of us was injured, but we wasted no time getting back down to the 1st floor! We were really very lucky, as glass flew all over the place.

I was worried to death about Kenny. *Was he safe, or not!?* Soon he arrived back at the 'Y,' though, safe and sound! (*Whew! What a relief!*) The man in charge of the 'Y' suggested we go to and '*air-raid*' *shelter* close-by, as theirs was full. So Ken, his buddies, and I walked a few blocks down the street to a church, which had an '*air-raid*' *shelter*. We were lucky to find that they had room for us! It was about 50 feet below the surface, with winding, spiral staircases. Reaching the bottom level, we found it was very nice. It had '*double-deck*' *bunks*, and *nurses* on duty. What struck me was it was very *clean*!

We stayed there all night, during which time we could feel the *vibrations* of the **bombs** being dropped! The next morning, after leaving the shelter, we found a total *square-block* demolished, just a few blocks from the 'Y' where I tried to nap the night before! Besides the '*air-raid*' on our convoy going over to England, this was my first taste of war, and the horrors that go with it.

The next day, a London newspaper read, *"last night's attack was the worst one, yet."* What a time to '*hit the town*!' Ironically, another paper's 'headline' read: "***Berlins Worst Night of Terror***!" While the Germans were bombing *London*, the RAF (Royal Air Force) was bombing *Berlin*!. On the very same night, with both sides reporting their worst night yet*!*

11

The Plane Effect

O N THE NIGHT the night mentioned above, that of January 21ˢᵗ of 1944, the British R.A.F launched the biggest and most awesome bombing raid on the city of Berlin, Germany as of that date! According to a *front-page article* from ***The Daily Mail*** of London for Saturday, January 21ˢᵗ, 1944, some **2,300 *tons*** of explosives were dropped on the city, and some **3,000** Berliners were *killed*!

Ironically, as I said, on the very same night, the Germans launched their largest air attack on the city of London! What a coincidence! That was a powerful attack, too! As I've told you, I was caught up in it! My brother and I just happened to be on an over-night pass in London that night. A dangerous and *'hectic night'* it turned out to be, indeed! (*I was just so glad that my brother Kenny was not hit that night, being out and about town as he was. We were both very lucky, with so many others hurt or killed.*)

The array of *gigantic flood-lights* dancing back and forth across the dark, blue, night sky, trying to catch in their beams the enemy attackers, so their powerful *'ack-ack' (anti-aircraft)* guns could blast them out of the sky was *awesome*, an *awesome sight*. Sometimes they *succeeded*. I'm sure this was *also* the scene over Berlin that night, in *reverse roles*, of course, as the R.A.F unleashed *their* attack! You could see approximately what section of the city the bombs were hitting; and you could feel the vibrations of the *giant 'block-buster' bombs* as they *hit* and *exploded* – *even deep down in an air-raid shelter* some 5 *stories below the surface!* It was very *frightening*, even *down-there*, where you were protected. It was hard to imagine what *sheer terror* and *pandemonium* it must have been for folks stuck at the *surface*, actually enduring the *full strength* of each blast! I could only imagine how many were killed.

As I said, Ken and I were in London on that particular night and experienced the *frightening effect* of being caught in an *air-raid*. This gave us a real *appreciation* for what the poor London *civilians* had been enduring! The next day, we wondered around London to see some of the *damage*. It was *awesome, to say the least*! There were *bombed-out buildings* everywhere. Just 2 blocks from where we stayed in the *air-ra*id shelter, a complete *square-block* was *destroyed* and lay in *ruins*! Buildings all *around* the area of a bomb blast would get a lot of damage from '*concussion*.' Windows would be *blown out, roofs blown off, holes put in the pavement and sidewalks.*

To think that this went on practically *every night* during this period is hard to believe, *but it did!* Even harder to believe was that the British carried on their usual *night-life* activity as if *nothing even happened*! They had *adapted* to living in a *war-zone* and did *not* let it bother them. What *courage* and *grit*! Their prime-minister, Winston Churchill, gave them much *encouragement* by broadcasting constantly that, *'We shall not be beaten! We will survive! Keep your nose to the grind-stone! We shall prevail!'* The British people, as well as the whole world, simply *loved* Winston; and he gave them the *courage, determination*, and *leadership* they needed to endure and persevere through those *terrible* times. Even with the American troops in Britain, the British people needed a source of encouragement and strength and leadership, as they were being bombed *relentlessly*.

Speaking about the aircraft, the military planes, I remember the gross feeling of *security* whenever a fighter plane flew over our position . . . (as long as it was one of *ours*! . . . otherwise, a feeling of gross *terror*!). Air power, the air-war, played an important role, and was an important part of World War II, both in Europe and in the Pacific. Though all aircraft was then still *propeller-driven*, long before the age of the *jet-engine*, they delivered a *deadly impact* when flying in *large numbers*.

The **P-51** fighter was always a sight to see. It was considered the *fastest, most maneuverable* plane in the world, at the time. I saw many *'dog-fights'* involving the P-51. The **P-38** was also a beautiful *twin-fuselage* plane that was very common. Each plane had its own particular *sound*, and we were soon able to distinguish between German and Allied planes; and then between each individual *type* of plane, each having its own distinctive sound. My brother Kenny was an *armourer*, servicing the P-51 fighters.

The German **V-1** and **V-2** *pilot-less* rocket-planes weren't considered airplanes to the *Germans*. They were considered *rockets*. They had wings, so they appeared to be *planes*; but, they were *pilot-less*, so they were more like *rockets*. We called them *'buzz bombs'* because they made a strange *buzzing sound* as they flew overhead. They traveled in a perfectly *straight line*, not like a plane, which *maneuvered around*, turning here and there. Many nights we watched them go overhead on their way to London, their *favorite target*! It was the R.A.F. versus the Luftwaffe for the Battle of Britain.

For months *before* D-Day, the American air forces were bombing targets in Germany, coordinating their strategy with the British Royal Air Force. Together, they *leveled* many targets, including *factories, bridges and many other storage and production sites in many strategic areas*. Leipzig, Munich, and Berlin were the largest, though only a few of the cities hit. Despite all the *demolition*, the Germans kept going. Unbeknownst to us at the time, they had many *underground facilities* to manufacture *weapons* and many other *much needed supplies*. The Germans were always very *clever* and *hard-fighting*, a *blunt* and *lethal* enemy.

The **B-17** and the **B-24** were the *newest* and *best* bombers in the air, and both were the *pride* of the U.S. Air Force! The B-24 was a *huge* airplane with a *gigantic wingspan* and a *bomb pay-load un-heard of* at the time! *Both* were used on attacks over Germany. Imagine the *horror* of hundreds and hundreds of *tons* of bombs being dropped on your city, for *days and weeks on end*, as in London! Imagine the *horror* of being a pilot or crewman being shot at, or *shot-down* and knowing you were diving to your *death*! (Or, at very best, that you were diving to *demolition behind enemy lines*, where you were *sure to be captured*.) These were *brave* men, and they made a big difference in the war effort.

12

Tea in Bristol

ON ONE OF my visits to Bristol, England, I stopped at the *lunch-counter* at the rail-station. When ordering, I thought I would try the *English tea*, which was a **mistake**! They know *nothing* of making tea, *absolutely nothing*! Anyway, I ordered a glass of tea and asked for some *sugar – another mistake!* The waitress was a young '*whipper-snapper*,' and she replied, in her English '*broage*, *"Don't you know there's a war on*! *We don't have any sugar!*" My reply: **"What the hell do you think I'm doing over here anyway!? . . . sight-seeing!?"**

13

From 'Pub' to 'Tub'

O N ONE OF the visits Ken & I took to Bristol, on an *'over-night pass,'* we encountered a *little problem!* After *'hitting a few pubs,'* we thought it was about time to check-out *lodging* for the night. After all, Bristol was like London, full of G.I.s, making accommodations sometimes hard to find. To our dismay, all the YMCA s and such were all *"full-up."* Finally, we came across a sign reading "Rooms to Let," but upon inquiring, we found they, too, were *"full-up!"*

We were about to walk away, when the lady who answered the door said, *"Wait, you 'Yanks!' I may have something else."* She had probably noticed the *disappointmen*t on our faces when she said, *"Sorry, we're full-up!"* We thought she was a little *'loose-in-the-rafters'* when she said, *"You 'Yanks' may sleep in the bath-tub!"* *"What did you say!?"* we asked, as we looked at each other in *shocked amazement,* wanting to *laugh aloud!*

Whether it was true of all the rooming-houses I don't know, but in her place, the *bath-tubs* were in *separate rooms,* toilets in others. After looking the situation over, we thanked her, and left. *(After all, she was trying to oblige us.)* As a last resort, we headed back to the train depot and the *hard, wooden benches* in the *waiting-room!*

After napping for a while, I awoke feeling somewhat *'fuzzy,'* so I headed out into the night air. After breathing deeply for a while, I felt somewhat better. Ken noticed how I felt and was quite *concerned,* as we both had to be back to our respective bases the next morning. But we had to catch different trains.

I told him not to worry, that everything would be OK. Come morning, the sunlight coming through the skylights woke me, *just in time, as my train pulled in shortly afterwards*! Everything worked out ok. We both got back on time. I sometimes wonder how the *'tub'* would have worked out!

14

London by Cab

BROTHER KEN AND I were in England some *8-months* before D-Day. He was stationed about 30 miles north of London, while I was about 100 miles to the southwest. He got to go into London quite often, while I was there just twice, both times with him meeting me there.

On this particular occasion, we decided to take a *tour* of London by cab and 'see *the sites*!' We told the *'cabbie'* to take us to all the major places. The English cabs were quite *'roomy,'* with large windows, compared to American cabs. Ken and I sat in the back seat comfortably while the driver *pointed-out* this place and that place, . . . place after place, for a couple of hours. We saw the **London Bridge**, a *masterpiece* of engineering, and very *majestic* looking! Why we didn't ask him to drive us over it, I don't know. Then there was '*Big Ben*,' the famous clock-tower – so *huge* and *stately* looking! The English architecture was really something – *very beautiful!*

We toured London for quite some time, form one section to another. The *'cabbie'* was very informative, enlightening us on the historic architecture of the city, and its history, dating so far back. But the highlight of our grand tour was **Winchester Cathedral**! **Wow**! *What a place! It was so huge and ornate*! We went through the inside and spent quite some time there. *Talk about architecture – that had to be some of the most beautiful in the world!* There was so much *ornate 'molding': up and down the corners, ceiling 'molding,' baseboard 'molding'* . . . all in **solid gold**! The floors were *marble* and *ornate tile – simply beautiful!* The **chandeliers** were *incredible – so huge, and with so many sparkling **crystals**!*

What I didn't know, and what surprised me the most, was to learn that in the walls and under the floors were *buried **English royalty**!* Their names and titles were engraved in gold: from *Princes* and *Princesses* to *Kings* and *Queens*!

Our guide, the *'cabbie,'* also timed it so that we could see the *'changing-of-the-guard'* at **Buckingham Palace**! Now *that* was really *something to see!* The soldiers wore very *tall, black hats (probably 3 or 4 feet tall!)*, and red and white uniforms (*if I remember right!*), and marched in *rigid, marching steps*, with rifle in one hand, saluting with the other, in such *precise rhythm*! So *dramatic*! The guards are constantly on duty protecting the palace in shifts **24-hours a day, 7 days a week!**

With *'tip'* included, we paid the driver 5 pounds. This was equivalent to $25.00 in our American money! It was worth every penny of it! We enjoyed the entire tour very much.

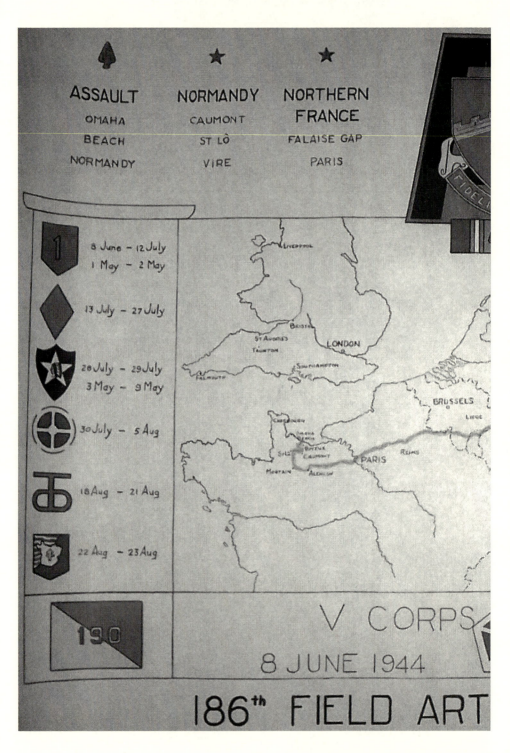

ASSAULT

NORMANDY

NORTHERN
FRANCE

OMAHA
BEACH
NORMANDY

CAUMONT
ST LÒ
VIRE

FALAISE GAP
PARIS

8 June – 12 July
1 May – 2 May

13 July – 27 July

28 July – 29 July
3 May – 9 May

30 July – 5 Aug

18 Aug – 21 Aug

22 Aug – 23 Aug

LIVERPOOL

BRISTOL
ST ANDRES
TAUNTON
FALMOUTH
SOUTHAMPTON
LONDON

BRUSSELS
LIEGE

CHERBOURG
OMAHA
BEACH
ST LÔ
CAUMONT
MORTAIN
ALENÇON
PARIS
REIMS

V CORPS
8 JUNE 1944

186ᵗʰ FIELD ART

Battle Campaign Map for our

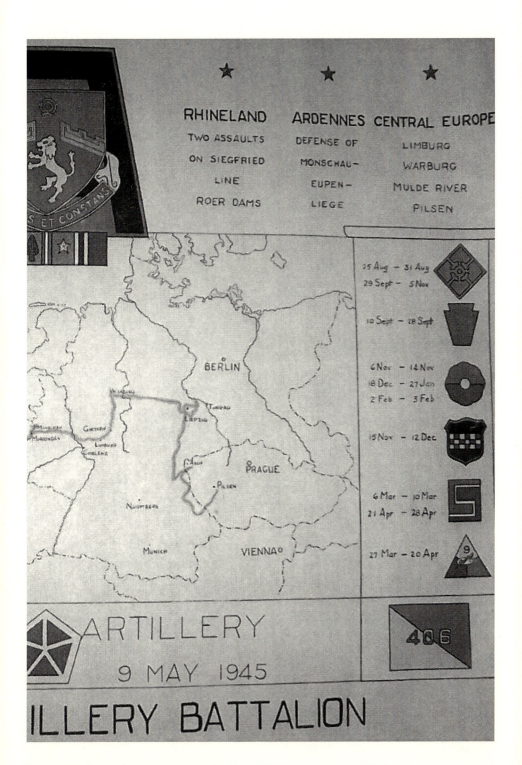

186th Field Artillery Battalion

15

Ike Visits

PRIOR TO THE invasion of France, **General Dwight D. Eisenhower** *('Ike')* and his *top – brass* visited our base (*St. Audries Camp*) situated at Somerset Shire, UK.

We had advance notice of this, and were ordered to *'spruce-up'* our living-quarters as well as *the person!* This was an all-day job: *scrubbing floors, dusting walls, etc.* The next day, at about noon, *'Ike'* arrived.

The area outside the barracks was *too small* for all to assemble at once, so we were ordered to stay *inside*, and see what we could by looking out the windows! We were all *thrilled* to get a glimpse of the *'chief,'* as 'Ike' was *admired* by everyone. He and his entourage of officers stood there in the circle of the courtyard and looked all around, pointing to this and that. Soon he made a *speech*, which was sent out over the loudspeaker system. It went something like this:

'I stand before you today to honor and respect you, and to inform you that you are about embark on an honorable and grave mission, from which some of you may not return. My heart goes with you. May God bless and be with you as you venture on the journey ahead.'

The Chaplain then said a prayer and wished us the best, with God's speed.

16

Omaha Beach

BEFORE I REALIZED it, the day came that we were to depart. We loaded at Falmouth, England, on *2 LSTs (Landing Ship Tanks; I was on #212)* consisting of *539 men*, with *attachments* from the *Service Battery, B-Battery, and a medical attachment*, 12 *Howitzers*, and *77 vehicles*, and *heavy equipment*. All of this to make-up *one* artillery battalion! *I just couldn't believe the size of the Armada of ships before my eyes! As far as I could see, there were ships of all classes and sizes!* The most *awesome*, the *huge battleship*, with their giant *16-inch guns* blasting away, '*salvo*' after '*salvo*,' and *rolling* '*side-to-side*' as their guns *recoiled*! What a support of confidence, as we were about to *invade* **Omaha Beach**! At the same time, *Cruisers, Destroyers*, and small '*gun-boats*' were all *firing away* at their targets on land!

The sky was completely full of *aircraft: bombers and fighters*, on *one level*, flying *in* to meet the enemy, and *at another level (a higher level), flying back* to England to *re-load* and *return*! This routine went on *from dawn to dusk, for days and days on end!*

The '*hottest*' piece of *real-estate* in the world in 1944 was, *undoubtedly, Normandy, France . . .* **Omaha Beach**, in particular.

D-Day is looked upon as the **6ᵗʰ of June**, but, actually, it was just the start of many D-Days to follow. The 1ˢᵗ Infantry Division *('The Big Red One')* took the *'brunt'* of the attack. Our battalion, the 186ᵗʰ Field Artillery (F.A.), was *attached* to the 1ˢᵗ Infantry Division as part of the *initial assault* forces on Omaha Beach. The fearless infantry-man is always the first to experience **'hell.'** The *1ˢᵗ* lost many courageous men on Omaha Beach on D-Day. On all 5 beaches *(Utah, Omaha, Gold, Juno, and Sword), many thousands lost their lives!*

The beach was heavily *mined*, and with many *barbed-wire barricades*. Our Battalion was part of the *assault force* of the *3ʳᵈ wave* of troops to *'hit'* the beach. At the designated time, the *'gang-plank'* door of our ship flopped open, with a big splash as it landed. The waters ran *red* with the *blood* of the 1ˢᵗ Infantry men, *lying on the beach*, many even *floating in the sea!*

My heart *pounded!* I was *scared to death*, and *mad as hell! Mad at that S.O.B. Hitler!*

Enemy artillery was *pounding* the beach! Our battleships were *responding!* The enemy infantry had pretty-well been *eliminated* from the beach. Enemy artillery, *'shrapnel,'* and *mines* were our biggest concerns at the moment. To our right flank, a *narrow road* had been made by the *infantry* and the *army engineers*, undoubtedly, at a *high price* in terms of *lives*, so that *we* could land our *vehicles*.

Our *Howitzers, half-tracks, and trucks of all sizes* had to have a safe road to travel over the beach. Our *Howitzers* were needed desperately, as well as other *artillery units* and *tanks* to follow! Next to the *tanks*, the *artillery guns* were probably the most *feared* by the enemy; and for good reason, since our *Howitzers* could fire a **97 lb.** *shell* some **9 and ½ miles!**

Our unit was ordered to the vicinity of *Russey*, to reinforce the fire of the 33ʳᵈ Artillery Battalion by the commanding General of the 1ˢᵗ infantry artillery. As we passed a farm-house, suddenly some *rifle-shot* came from a big tree near by. Riding in a 5-ton truck, on the *end-seat, I fired my carbine*, as did several others. A *body* fell from the tree. It was later rumored that it was a *lady* sniper*! I often wonder . . .*

(Our unit was always under the command of the division to which we were attached. We were V Corp artillery, meaning that we could be ordered to go where ever needed, from one division to another. Each division has many

artillery battalions, but they stay within the perimeters of that division. Only V Corps artillery was mobile between divisions. This is why I say we were the 'Phantom Battalion!')

At this point, the Germans had been *pushed back* a few miles from the beach. Our next position was near *Cattun*. It was June 8th, and on the 10th, the battalion's 2 liaison planes arrived from England ... *'touching-down'* at the *'crash-strip'* near *Vierville*. Also at this point, the 103rd A.A.A. (Anti-Aircraft Battalion) joined in our position. It was customary for us to have an AAA unit, as we were often *attacked* by enemy air-craft.

Again, we were *displaced* to a *new position* near *Le Vivier*. Yet, on the *same day* we moved to the vicinity of *Selouet*. The enemy *resistance* in this area was quite *fierce*, and we were kept *very busy!* Persistence *'paid-off,'* though. By the 12th, we had succeeded in *displacing* the enemy. The next day, liaison was established with the 7th Armored Division artillery of the British 2nd Army. The battalion was assigned the additional mission of giving general support to the porters of the front of the right flank of the British 2nd Army within the reach of our guns. Again, our guns having a range of *9 and ½ miles, delivering a shell of about 97 lbs.!)*

It was on June 14th that the remaining part of our battalion arrived on Omaha Beach: *86 men, and 48 vehicles in all*. They were soon to join the rest of the outfit.

Each time we changed position, *sometimes 2 or 3 times-a-day*, my job was to lay *phone-wire* from the *command-post* to the 4 *Howitzers*. There were 3 of us to do the job. There were several of us who *'manned'* the Command-Post *phones*. We *alternated* doing this. We relayed the commands *exactly* as they came from headquarters. When the *phone rang*, and the voice said, **"Fire-Mission!"** – *We went into action!* Immediately, a *'crank'* of the *phone rang the phones* at all the guns. **"Report-in!"** *I would say, and each gun would* **acknowledge, "Gun # 1! Gun # 2! Gun # 3! Gun # 4!"**

"Stand ready!" *would be the next command.* **"Fire mission!** ... *Elevation: 'so-and-so!' range: 'so-and-so!' powder-charge: 'so-and-so!' All guns report-in when ready!"*

"Gun one ready! Gun two ready! Gun three ready! Gun four ready!" *they would reply.*

"Fire!"

*With this command, they **all fired at once**, and the **ground shook!**/* Under favorable flying conditions, our *reconnaissance plane* would be *'aloft'* *relaying back* the *results*: *either a direct hit, or a near miss.* By now we were gaining a reputation of being a *'crack'* outfit – *always close to the mark!*

On the afternoon of June 13th, the *'command-phone' rang.* I happened to be on duty at the time. The orders were: ***"Shift trails 90-degrees to the left!"*** I was *shocked!* We had never received such an order! I did something a *'lowly' Corporal never does – question an order!* But the Lieutenant on duty *agreed.* The command was repeated in a *stranger* voice: ***"Shift trails 90-degrees to the left! Report when ready!"***

I relayed the message to the guns. The orders aroused *similar doubts* in the Sergeants in charge of each gun; but in a matter of minutes, the guns all *reported back, "Ready!"* I relayed the message back to headquarters. They sent the *firing* commands back, and soon we began *firing!* We had never had a situation like this before.

It seems that the British 7th Armored Division was *'bundled'* down by the Germans, and they called for *help!* Our battalion and 3 units were in the vicinity within firing range.

We were in support of the 1st Division at the **Battle of St. Lo** . . . *which was quite an ordeal.* This was our next major battle. *We kept firing all the rest of the day, and practically all night! Our guns really lit-up the skies! We never stopped firing.* The next day, was *very heavy,* too. By morning, one of our Howitzer *gun barrels* was *'fired-out,'* (*i.e. burned out)!* The barrel needed *replacing!*

Normally, the remedy would be to *take the gun* back to *ordinance* battalion to be replaced, usually 5 miles to the rear. But on this occasion, the *ordinance* was ordered to *come to our position* to *replace the barrel!* This gives some indication of the ***emergency*** of our mission, and the ***severity*** of this battle! The British were *cornered!* Our mission continued into the night of the 2nd day before the British could *withdraw.*

In between my shifts at the command-post, I curled-up in my *'fox-hole,'* and *tried to sleep!* Imagine, *with 4 Howitzers blasting* away *continuously,* and the ground *shaking!* But I did *actually sleep* for a while, because I was *completely drained!*

The British were *very grateful.* The *very next day,* unannounced, they came to 'A' Battery to thank us *in person* . . . *lead by none-other than*

Field Marshall Montgomery himself! This fact is *un-documented,* but he *shook-hands* with *each and every one of us,* and said, *"Thank you,"* . . . calling us by rank. Later, we received a *'commendations'* signed by the *(other)* commanding officer of the British 7th Armored Division.

It was a known fact that the Field Marshal and General *'Ike'* didn't get along. Jealousy prevailed because Montgomery thought that he should have been chosen to be the Supreme Allied Commander instead of *'Ike,'* and had different strategies of the war. Montgomery was next in command, though. Had something happened to General Eisenhower, he would have been in full command.

'Ike' was a *'desk general,'* and he thought that Montgomery should have been, too; but *Monty* was a *'field general,'* a *'tank man'* at heart. He was, evidently, with the 7th Armored Division when they got corned by the Germans at *'Villers-Bocage salient'* during this battle. Maybe the Germans knew that Montgomery was there and fought harder to capture or kill him.

'Monty' was in many *serious* situations; the next noted being his *retreat* from Dunkirk, North Africa. He was routed by General Rommel, *"the Desert Fox,"* his German counter-part.

During the month of **June, 1944**, our battalion fired **5,036 shells**, at a total of **3,198 targets**! The **targets** included: *counter-attacks, counter-battery, machine-guns, observation-posts, mortars, personnel, strong-points, vehicles, tanks, harassing-rounds, and registration and check points.*

We were quite active during the month of **July**, too, on the move supporting many units. Besides the 1st Infantry, there was the 5th Infantry Division, the 2nd Armored, the 35th Infantry, and 2nd U.S. Infantry. The field-artillery units that we supported were: the 33rd, the 19th, the 406th, the 38th, and the 17th. These were all within the areas of *La Vieille,* beside *Bouvy,* and *Gosville,* France.

It's plain to see why we were the Phantom Battalion . . . *always on the move, sometimes occupying 2 or 3 positions in 1, 24-hour period!* At each position, the guns had to be *'dug-in,'* phone-wire *laid,* fox-holes *dug.* (Each man was responsible for digging his own fox-hole, after getting the guns in position and ready to fire. The fox-holes were used for *'cover,'* in case of enemy attack, whether by artillery or planes, as well as to *sleep* in.)

This month, Battery 'C' was 'strafed' by an enemy ME 109, evidently just a stray plane, causing no casualties or other damage. Another statistic: our 2 *'spotter'* planes flew a total of *97 missions*, for a total of *110 flying-hours*. We fired **5,868** rounds of *ammo* in July. By this, you can tell that the ordinance battery attached to our rear-echelon was kept busy following us and keeping us supplied with ammo!

17

Tasting of the Wine

IT WAS DURING a time when the war was sort of *standing still . . . somewhere* in France. A *'water-detail'* of *2 men and a Jeep* usually went back to the *'water-point,'* whenever necessary, to get the *drinking water.* On this day, the detail came back to camp – *but with no water!* . . . **Wine** filled the 5-gallon cans instead!

The *'detail'* had come across a French *wine-cellar,* and decided to treat all of us guys! Considering that none of the enlisted men had had any alcohol in a long time, it was a treat all right!

It was a really *warm day,* and the wine tasted good. Personally, I never really cared for wine, so I didn't drink very much. . . . *Lucky for me*! After a couple of hours of *hot sun* and *cold wine,* the men were *passing-out all over the place*!

Soon the *phone rang: "Fire-mission!" (Oh, no!)* I *hated* to repeat the command to the guys at the guns. They performed their duties *as best they could under the circumstances.* But soon, the Colonel came *racing* into the area in his jeep, from *headquarters battery*! Some of the guys were *staggering around*; others were *'propped-up'* against the trees; some were *'passed-out!'*

The Colonel was **furious**! When he received the *'accuracy-report'* from the *'spotter'* plane, he knew something was *terribly* wrong! (*After all*, again, by this time, we were known as a *'crack'* outfit, and our *reputation* was *excellent*.) As punishment, the Colonel *'broke'* everyone who was *noticeably drunk* by 1 rank. *I was lucky that I didn't care much for wine!*

Me and Tom

18

Cognac

IN FRANCE THERE are *vineyards everywhere.* They grow *grapes* there like the farmers here at home grow *corn* or *soybeans.* Besides *wine* though, they are also known for making *Cognac* from the wine. And it is *potent stuff!* . . . I mean real *'fire-water!'*

One time, *'just for the 'heck of it,'* a couple of the guys in my unit poured a *gallon-or-two of Cognac* into the **gas-tank** of a jeep! . . . Just to see what would happen . . . *And it worked!* . . . The motor *'purred like a kitten!'* The jeep ran just *fine!*

Thank God I didn't like the stuff and couldn't drink very much of it! . . . Just think of your *stomach!*

19

Paris

O N THE NIGHT of August 1st, 1944, while in support of the 35th Infantry Division, our battalion area *was attacked by enemy bombers*, mostly in Battery-C area. Battery A was not affected. In the C area, the *3 wire-men* on duty worked and repaired the communication lines *while the bombing was still going on.* For their courage, later, they were awarded the **Bronze Star**.

Battery-B observer, while on mission with the infantry at the *front-line*, and in the direct line with a series of enemy *tanks*, conducted *'observation firing'* on the enemy, allowing us to: *knock-out enemy tanks, kill enemy personnel, and just about destroy their entire 'strong-hold' in the area.*

At another battle, the battalion fired almost continuous *'night-firing,'* contributing to the *'closing-of-the-gap'* and virtual destruction of the enemy forces at that location.

On August 24th, we had a *march-order,* to a *'bivouac' area (a rest area),* 120 miles away, near *Metz-Laville,* France. Our battalion liaison team, and the 17th U.S. Infantry combat team they were assisting, was considered the *first to enter Paris!* On the march to the *'bivouac,'* we passed **General Patton's** 3rd Army tanks, with their infantry *riding on the tanks!* I had heard the story before . . . that his soldiers had to wear *neck-ties*! I never believed it until that day! There they were, riding atop the tanks – ***wearing neck-ties***!

Since our battalion was being attacked more frequently by enemy aircraft, a call for more AAA protection was issued by the Corps Commander. The 462 AAA Battalion was shifted to our position. Around the 20th of August, due to the increased demand for *artillery-fire* in the Falaise-Argentan *('Falaise-Gap')* area, our ammunition supply was expended to the point that we could no longer answer the call for *'fire-missions!'* The Colonel was ***furious***! This had never happened before! It was a simple case of supply and demand, so our *'fire-missions'* were relayed to other battalions in the area.

During **August**, our battalion occupied positions in **12** *different areas*! In one incident, the AAA unit attached to our battalion *captured 7 German soldiers, killing 2*. On another day, our battalion reconnaissance party *encountered a company of German infantry consisting of 70 men and 2 officers with a full compliment of arms and equipment*. Through their quick efforts, *they captured the whole lot!*

August was quite an eventful month. Although we supported only 4 different units, we were in *12 areas*, with some *'night firing,'* also. The *'Falaise-Gap'* was the big battle. In one 2-day period, we *fired* almost *continuously* on a column of enemy infantry, inflicting *heavy damage*, with all firing being observed by our air and ground observers. In another instance, we pretty well *destroyed* or *dispersed* a large column of *tanks, horse-drawn vehicles and marching troops*. On another occasion, a *3-mile column* of enemy transport and troops was hit by battalion volleys, under the direction of forward observers! In each of these cases, the damage was tremendous!

One of the most *dreaded* units in the Army is the *artillery*, because *its fire-power* is so *tremendous*! We were gaining momentum as a *'top-notch'* unit.

Up until this point, I had been getting very well accustomed to working in the *command firing post* of my battery. I was somewhat surprised to be kept in that position after the incident where I *questioned a direct order (the Montgomery case)*! Since I was not *reprimanded* for this, I assumed that I was right to do so, or, at least, they understood *why* I did so.

I forgot to mention that, even though the war was going on at a vigorous pace, the mail system did a good job keeping up with us. *Usually, it took a month to receive mail.* The folks back-home mailed packages regularly; and sometimes I would get *4 or 5 packages* of *'goodies'* at one time! And so would some of the other guys. We always shared them. I remember receiving a package with a *birthday cake* in it! It was pretty much just *crumbs*, but it was *delicious*; and it was baked by *Mom*!

Getting back to statistics, in **August of 1944**, we fired *4,872 rounds* of *ammo*! On *1 day alone*, August 19ᵗʰ, we expended *1,126 rounds*! Again, we had the ordinance company *come to our position* and replace *2 gun-barrels*. With such *continuous* firing, it's surprising that *all 4 guns* weren't burned-out! All this happened at the **Battle of the 'Falaise-Gap.'** We supported the following units during this month: the 35ᵗʰ Infantry Division, the 406ᵗʰ F.A. Group, the 90ᵗʰ U.S. Infantry Division, and the 12ᵗʰ Infantry Combat Team of the 4ᵗʰ U.S. Infantry Division.

The month of August was an *exhausting* month, and we had been in action *continuously* since Omaha Beach. Now our battalion was awarded and *R&R (Rest & relaxation) of 5 days*! We were still in France, somewhere south of Paris. All men were offered the opportunity to visit the *'French Riviera.'* I thought, *"French Riviera? What's that?"* I had never heard of that before; so, I didn't go. Later, I found out that I missed something *special*. I knew it was a *beaching* area, and since I didn't swim, it didn't appeal to me. Still, I enjoyed the frequent, *hot showers* and being a little *lazy*!

On another occasion, I could have gone to a U.S.O. performance to see **Bob Hope**! For some reason that I don't remember, *I declined*. This I *regretted*, for he was one of my favorites.

After 5 days of R&R and lots of dreaming, it was pretty hard *getting 'back in the grind'*.

Now it was another month. On September 5ᵗʰ, 4 German soldiers were captured near our position. They were evacuated. On the 6ᵗʰ, we took *'bivouac' (rest area)* in the vicinity of *Sevigny-LaForet*. Two days later, our orders were to go into 'bivouac' at Rienne, Belgium. A *'bivouac'* position is one you occupy *when there is no specific place that you are needed*. It is usually in a wooded area, camouflaged from enemy planes. After 2 more moves, we were in support of the 28ᵗʰ Infantry Division.

With a number of batteries, some major ones, behind us, we soon had our *'day of glory.'* The 186ᵗʰ *(Phantom Battalion)* marched through

Paris, France! (It is *documented* that the 38th Cavalry was the *first* to enter Paris. The 186th was *attached* to the 38th at this time, so we were *right there with them*.)

*What a day! All of **Paris** was out to greet us!... With wreaths and necklaces of flowers, and banners reading: "Viva la Americans!"... "Viva la Yankees!"... And, if you were lucky enough to be walking, with hugs and kisses! (I was not walking, though. I was riding in the back of a 5-ton truck.) The Parisians were just **ecstatic**!... **Shouting** and **screaming** at the tops of their voices!... They were so glad to be liberated!* They were so *appreciative* of our efforts. They were *overjoyed*, and they were *showing it!* This *was a wonderful treat, to be welcomed so warmly. It lifted the spirits of everyone in the convoy, and reminded us of what we were fighting for. It encouraged us to more victory, and it is a scene I will never forget.*

We went right by the **Eiffel Tower** and the **Arc de Triumph**!... *What beautiful sights!* At least Hitler hadn't destroyed *these*! *(He had occupied the city before us, you know!)* I'm sure he must have been equally impressed. I guess he thought that someday, they, and all of Europe, would be his *forever... all* the beautiful pieces of architecture, monuments, buildings, and churches across Europe ... *all* of the beautiful cities ... and *control* over *all of the people and armies!*... All to be subject to his *absolute command. After all, he was going to conquer all of Europe, including England, so he thought.* If we, the United States, hadn't entered the war when we did, he may very well have *succeeded.* Undoubtedly, with his allies of Italy and Japan, he would have conquered the *entire earth* if he could have. What an *outrageous*, military **mad-man!**

20

September to December 1944

ON SEPTEMBER 11TH, the orders from the division headquarters were to move into position at Binsfield, Luxemburg. Twelve German soldiers were captured by the 461st AAA outfit. The next day, we were sent in support of the 107th F.A. Battalion . . . back in Belgium, in the vicinity of *Quiren*. Some of the battalion was under harassing mortar fire. We were now with the 4th U.S. Infantry Division, re-enforcing the fire of the 44th F.A. Battalion.

I remember that this was the area where you could stand and put your feet in 3 different countries in a matter of seconds! *Belgium, Luxembourg and Germany all border each other at 1 point!* I remember, too, that this was the location of a *fierce fight* between the enemy and the 4th Infantry! This is the only time I remember being *so close* to an infantry, with their *mortars* firing from *behind* us! (*Mortars only have a range of approximately 1 mile! Our guns fired a distance of some 9and1/2 miles!*) I guess they knew what they were doing!

Ironically, after the war, when I was working on the railroad, I became acquainted with a *co-worker* who just happened to be one of the *infantry-men involved in this fight!* Again, what a *small* world!

From this point, we *'stepped'* back into Germany, this time to support the 109th Infantry Division in operations against the **"*Siegfried Line*,"** the supposed *'impregnable'* line of defense! This line consisted of *large, concrete, cone-shaped obstructions,* supposedly placed in a manner where no one could pass over or through them, even with *tanks*! But our *'Phantom Battalion'* did! We *blasted* our way through! A 155mm shell at *'point-blank'* range will go through just about *anything*!

October was somewhat *slower* time for the 186th. Winter was beginning to set in; and, *in a way,* this was welcomed. This gave us a chance to make some *community fox-holes*! To make these, we *(3 or 4 men)* would dig a *square* hole, *some 6 to 8 feet square,* and *some 4 feet deep.* After cutting *tree-branches* some *4 to 5 inches in diameter,* we would use them to form a roof over the hole, on top of which we laid smaller, leafy branches. Then, on top of this, we would shovel enough dirt to hold them down. It was big enough to be *comfortable,* yet small enough to be *warm.* This was a welcome change.

During these *'slow'* periods, the battalion would fire *'harassing missions,'* just to let the enemy know the war was *still on*! They, in return, would *'acknowledge'* our action. We considered them to be *'poor shots,'* so we didn't have to worry too much. (*Although, I do remember some 'duds' that were quite close!*)

I believe I mentioned earlier that our commanding officer was quite *strict.* I want to say here that that was an *understatement*! This incident happened during one of our *'slow'* periods. I was *not* involved, but I *witnessed* what took place.

Four of our men came upon a *live calf.* Most all of the animals were dead from *'shell-shock.'* At least 1 of our men, I know, was a *'farm boy.'* It so happened that none of us had had any good meat for a *very* long time, let alone *freshly butchered* meat! They *killed* and *butchered* the calf, and they were going to treat everyone in our battery! The captain *'got wind'* of what was going on, and he put a *stop* to it immediately! He ordered the men involved to dig a hole and *bury* the whole thing! He said that the animal didn't belong to us, so we couldn't have the meat, *even after it had been butchered! Oh, yes, the captain was well liked!*

About this time, the *mail* caught up with us again. Besides the very welcome letter from all the folks back home, I received more *great packages*! As I opened them, I was *imagining* and *hoping* for *certain* things. I always got at least 2 boxes at a time. Mom and my sisters really made sure that my brother Ken and I were not forgotten! This was *always* a *treat*!

Besides the weather turning colder, we were getting a lot of *rain*, too. The *mud* was something to *contend* with! Sometimes, one of our trucks would get stuck and have to use their *wench*, which was attached to the front of each large truck. We didn't worry about the jeeps or 'half-tracks'.

Another good thing about '*slow*' time was that our '*kitchen-truck*' would catch up with us and serve *hot food and coffee!* Sometimes we lived on C and K rations for days or *weeks*, so you can imagine what a *treat* this was, even though it was still *Army food!*

Civilians Celebrating in the street!

This month of **October**, our outfit was mostly in Belgium, occasionally *'slipping'* back over into Germany for a *'spell'*. At the time, it was hard to believe that with the war still going, that the poor civilians, of mostly the small towns, would have anything to celebrate, short of the war itself *ending*; but, believe it or not, *they were always celebrating someone's birthday, or something else, having street dancing and women in traditional garb!* Both the people of Belgium and Germany had this custom.

Once in a while, when we were on the move, we would see a passing column of *tanks* – the *tank-men* deserved a *lot* of credit for their efforts, too – or, maybe another *artillery battalion, and sometimes a column of tired, walking, displaced civilians.* What a *sad sight* this would *always* be. *My heart went out to them!*

On October 1ˢᵗ, we moved into position at *Schmeiler*, Germany, with the 461 AAA Battalion attached. Our battalion was attached to the 406ᵗʰ F.A. Group in general support of the 4ᵗʰ Infantry. Everything was *quiet* in this area. *'Harassing missions'* were about all the *'missions'* we fired. On the 9ᵗʰ, we got orders to move to the vicinity of *Murringen*, Belgium.

October and **November** of **1944** were *quiet* times for the *whole front*. Being the *winter* was setting in, I guess the *high-command* took it easy for a while. But *little did they know* that it was due largely because the Germans were *taking advantage* of the weather and *building up their positions* for what was to be their *last attempt to win the war* – the **Battle of the Bulge**! *November* was one of the most *in-active* months of all. The battalion only fired slightly over **2,000** rounds of **ammo**! Little did we know what was about to happen!

'Mo' had some time to entertain us with his accordion. It was about all the *'cheering up'* we had. We had lots of time to *write letters home*, and *dream* of home a little bit. A German reconnaissance plane would fly over once in a while. An occasional German artillery shell would *'come in to say hello,'* and we would *'answer back'*. All these little things in a day's activity.

In mid-November, the *snow* began to *accumulate*, and the *temperatures* began to *drop*.

21

The Ravages of War

IT IS *SAD* that *long* before the *start* of World War II, the people of Europe couldn't have seen what was on the horizon. Since the inception of the war, they, and the rest of the world, no doubt, wished they would have seen what was about to happen, and somehow been able to stop it, long before it ever became a war. Here was Germany's young, new *idol*, Adolf Hitler, promising to return the *pride* of Germany by making it the *next great empire, exhorting near idyllic enthusiasm* amongst his followers as he spoke with such *furious force* and *wild fervor*, preaching *anti-Semitism*, anti-communism and *forcing* tens of thousands of young male countrymen into his army, an army that was, all too soon, going to doom Germany and Europe, and the United States and most of the world, to all out war, a war which would bring *devastation* and *atrocity* on a *scale never seen before*. It's *too bad* that none of the early *attempts* on Hitler's *life* were *successful!* One lucky hero could have saved Europe and *millions* upon *millions* of innocent lives, many of which were *poor, helpless civilians*.

Instead, a former *Corporal* of World War I became the *mad-man, lunatic, leader* of World War II. I believe he actually came *close to death* in WWI, and afterwards, while coming to power, several times; but, instead, he *survived, killing-off* his political opposition, rising to power, and *super-star* popularity, in Germany. He played on the still present *resentment* from the *war reparation penalties from WWI*, and the extreme *sadness* and *frustration* of the *Great Depression*, which had *hit Germany so hard*, to *rally* the German people to war, convincing them that the '*expansion*' of their German family by '*annexing*' their nearest neighbors was, *actually*, a *noble* action, meant to *unite* the German people as a whole. Austria and Czechoslovakia were '*annexed*,' as Britain and France settled on a policy of *appeasement*. When he invaded Poland, Britain and France *declared war* on Germany. In Poland he began *eliminating* the Jews, in huge *concentration camps*. His ultimate goal was, *obviously*, to take all of Europe, *including* England, and, indeed, rule an empire . . . *and then take America!*

The English Channel was the only thing that stopped him from taking England, after taking France without a struggle. Paris and two-thirds of France were given away when the French defenses failed. Winston Churchill, Britain and France began asking the U.S. for help as London started getting bombed. Hitler had earlier eased the tension somewhat by signing a '*non-aggression*' pact with their long-time enemy of Russia, but soon after that *violated* the treaty and *attacked* them, seeking to conquer the Soviet Union as well! This proved to be a *big mistake*, as Russia proved to be *too large* for him to take. Forcing all the *able-bodied* men from his conquered countries into the ranks of his *own* army, he pushed forward and *almost succeeded*, reaching the gates of Stalingrad. But with Stalin's '*scorched earth*' *policy*, and the West's '*lend, lease*' *program* he failed; but *millions* died. Without this *policy*, and *aid*, and the help of the *harsh* Russian *winter*, the Soviet Union may have fallen as well!

On the western front, Germany was *bombing* England almost *nightly*, and the English people were experiencing some of the *horrors* of war. Besides just the buildings and infrastructure, their *nerves* were taking the toll, the toll of the *terror* and *devastation* of war. After the attack on Pearl Harbor, the United States entered the war and started sending troops and supplies to Britain, as well as the Pacific, in preparation for the invasion of France, in *Operation Overlord*, beginning with the taking of the beaches of Normandy on *June 6th, 1944* . . . D-Day. The American command wanted to do this in *1943*, but Britain favored the idea of attacking Axis forces in *North Africa* as a *distraction*, instead, fearing that the American plan was *too straightforward and risky*. After *losing* to

Rommel in North Africa, the D-Day plan was finally accepted. Germany *suspected* this, and so started *fortifying* the coastal areas of France. Even though they didn't expect the invasion to be at *Normandy*, they had that area fortified *very strongly*. But, *on June 6th, 1944*, the *tide of the war changed*, with the *invasion* of Normandy. Although at a *very high cost*, the U.S. and its allies *succeeded* in taking the area and successfully driving the German army inland in a short time!

Soon the ravages of war were to be seen: *the helpless, innocent civilians!*... In this case, the French civilians: *men, women and children of all ages, who were seeing, feeling, and experiencing war and its terrible consequences*... *their homes being bombed-out, making them flea with only what they could carry on their backs!* They *wandered*, not knowing where they could find *safe shelter*. After consuming the *meager* amount of food they could *carry with them*, they never knew where or when their next meal would come. Worrying about the family members *lost* or *left behind* had to be a *heavy* load to carry. What about Grandma and Grandpa who were *too old and crippled* to *flea?* What were they to do? Stay and '*fend*' for themselves? Eat off the *land* and *pray?* Some survived and some did not, but *many* such *poor souls perished*. And many survivors found out, first-hand, that the American soldier was their *friend* and was there to help them, giving them *food*, a friendly *smile*, a *handshake*. These *made-up* for the difference in background and culture, and *crossed* the language barrier.

All across Europe, in: France, Belgium, Luxembourg, Germany... *it was the same story everywhere*. The surviving civilians were left *homeless* and were on the *move*... *seeking food, safety, shelter*. From time to time, when our battalion was enjoying a '*lull*' in the action, we would have our '*kitchen truck*' and *hot food*. If any civilians were around, they would gather near the *garbage cans* where we would scrape our plates. They would actually *eat out of the garbage cans*, using their *bare hands and fingers!* Many a soldier would leave a piece of *meat* or *bread* and hand it to them. They were so *grateful!* They would *smile, thanking* you in their language, *bowing their heads*. This was all *very hard to take*. You would have to see it to believe it!

In many cases, the small children had no shoes, raggedy clothes that were worn for days and weeks on end. Instantly, my thoughts went back home to the neighbor children. How *lucky* they were!

Entering Germany and seeing the same conditions as in France and Belgium made me feel just as bad, *except it was their leader's fault!*

As our armies advanced deeper inland, our command sat up '*displaced persons camps.*' Civilians who were completely *disoriented* were rounded up and given *food* and *shelter*. This was good to see. As time went on, there were *more camps* and *more people* to fill them. There were times I remember seeing *column after column* of homeless civilians walking towards the camps. Many had *grateful smiles* on their faces!

The very *worst*, and most *abominable*, civilian tragedies, were, of course, the *mass-murdering* of the Jewish people in the Nazi concentration camps. This seemed to be the *pet-project* of Hitler himself, administered and carried out by his specially appointed officers. The *rumor* was that one of Hitler's *parents* was Jewish, and for some reason he resented this to the extent that he ordered all the Jewish people to be killed. Regardless of age, health, wealth, or status – teacher, preacher, politician or whatever . . . *they were doomed!* What *terror* and *madness!* There are all sorts of new theories out about *why* he did this, but I don't think anybody really knows for sure.

The concentration camps where they gassed millions of Jews were, *obviously*, the most *terrible* and *atrocious* places and events of the war, perhaps of human history. No one really knew the *extent* of the *atrocities* until these camps began to be *liberated* at the end of the war. We have all seen the film footage – *shocking, despicable . . . unbelievable!* Thank goodness I was not involved with any of these camps! That would have been very difficult. I have heard stories of soldiers involved with their liberation, where some went *insane* over it! How awful.

In these camps, we now know, the people were *robbed* of their *belongings*, *stripped* of their *personal dignity*, *worked* to the *bone*, and, then, often *tortured* to *death*. The *mass-murdering* went on like *extermination*, done in *showers*, where *gas* poured out instead of *water!* All this just to satisfy the *twisted desire* of one *mad-man* who had come to power! How truly *sick* and *outrageous!* How *terribly sad!* He will surely *rot in hell forever* for that!

Thank goodness I did not have to deal with any of those situations. I found it very hard just to watch the *hungry, homeless civilians* who were *yet alive!* Thank God the United States *entered* the war and helped *free* Europe, or how many *more* would have been killed this way!? Thank God we *won* the war!

I often wonder how many of those *homeless civilians* ever *found* there *missing loved ones*, or were able to *return home* to their *actual households*, or were *at least* able to *find* and *bury* their dead relatives. Though I'm sure the figures cannot be exact, I've heard it said that as many as 100 *million* people *died* in this war, and as many as 150 *million* were left *homeless*! That would be approximately equal to the entire population of the United States at that time either being killed, or left homeless. This still seems *unbelievable* to me. How could this ever have happened? How did we ever survive?

I had *truly hoped* that the world would *learn* from these *terrible atrocities*, so that they would *never* happen again *anywhere* in the world; but, *sadly*, we have heard the term *'genocide'* mentioned *several times* in the past few decades. It is *truly disturbing* that this can *still happen*! If it does *continue* to occur, I hope that the world will *stand up valiantly*, as it did in WWII, and *stop* such evil *completely*, as this can simply *not* be *tolerated*! That is the *lesson* of WWII.

(Please excuse my *lack* of the story of the Pacific theatre, as I am largely *ignorant* of that, having been active only in Europe. There was much *intense fighting* there, *too*, and *many lives lost as well*; and the stories are *just as dramatic*, as we all well know.)

(Also, please *excuse* whatever *historical details* I may have gotten a *bit wrong*, or *slightly out of order*, for I am *not* a *historian*, and this is *not* meant to be a *history* of WWII, but rather my story and my best recollection of that time. I hope that I have gotten the basic WWII timeline right.)

22

A Stranger in Our Midst

AT THIS TIME, the war action for us was going at a very slow pace. Because of this, we were able to eat from the '*kitchen-wagon*,' an army truck equipped with cooking appliances, which they served meals out of. We were somewhere in France. One day, while we were standing in line in front of the '*chuck-wagon*,' we noticed a *stranger* in our midst.

He was very *noticeable*, because he was wearing *civilian* clothes. He was a *big* man in a tan *trench-coat*. He was sitting with the captain under a shade-tree in a folding chair. Someone said he was a friend of the captain, and his name was **Ernest Hemingway**! He was a war-correspondent newspaper reporter.

To me, the name meant nothing. I had never heard of him! I found out a little about him from the other guys. He had already written a book, or two. Later on, obviously, he became a very famous author, writing many more novels. Now, he is considered a *classic contemporary American author*! . . . *Taught in major colleges*! Since then, I've seen several major movies *based* on his books! (. . . the popular ones that all are familiar with: "*A Farewell to Arms*," "*For Whom the Bell Tolls*," "*The Sun also Rises"*) At the time, he was just a war-correspondent, covering the war in Europe.

It seems that he and the captains were friends, and from the same town – *Boston, I believe.* I didn't get to talk to him, but I was within a few feet of him. He seemed like an *'all right'* guy!

23

A Touching Moment

IT WAS SOMEWHERE in Belgium, in early *December 1944*, before the Battle of the Bulge. We had just arrived in this little town and decided it was time for *lunch*. In World War II, we had what was called *'C' rations*, and *'K' rations*. The difference I don't recall, but we lived quite regularly on both while we were on the move.

These *rations* were packed in small, heavily-waxed, cardboard boxes (to make them *water-proof*). Inside was what we called *'dog biscuits'* – a *hard, tasteless,* supposedly *'good for you'* biscuit. *No one liked them!* Also, there was a little, round 'tin of *potted ham*, which wasn't too bad! Then, there was a 3rd item, a *cheese* item packed in a *'tin.*

On this particular day, as we were sitting around *eating*, a small boy – probably 8 or 9 years old – came up to me. He had a *cute* little smile, and *big, friendly eyes . . .* which were *'eyeing-up'* my *food.* I gave him a *chocolate bar (also included in the rations)*, and he was *'thrilled to no end!* Before he left, I gave him a box of K rations, which *really thrilled him!* To this he said, *"I'll give this to 'Momma' from St. Nick!"* It was probably the only thing he had for her Christmas.

24

Lady in Black

IF POSSIBLE, ARTILLERY battalions travel at *night*, under the cover of darkness. One night stands out, in particular, in my mind. It was in Germany. As we were going down the road, the column of vehicles *'slowed-up'* a *'bit'* to *navigate a curve*. The moon was out as if for one purpose only – *to light-up the figure of an elderly lady, dressed in a long, black robe with a hood!*

Just as we turned the curve, she had her *head bowed* and her *hands clasped* in *prayer*, just standing there *solemnly* in the *moon-light, along the side of the road.* Was she praying for *us*, because we liberated her and her country? Or was she praying for her *family*, caught-up in the war somewhere? Or was she the *'Angel of Death?'*

For whatever reason, it was a *beautiful*, yet *ghastly* sight that I still vividly remember today.

25

'Mo'

THERE WAS A guy in our unit we all called *'Mo'.* He was a big, strapping, Polish guy. He was very *friendly.* Everyone liked him. He was very *talented,* too. He could really play the *accordion,* and the *piano.* He always had an accordion in his possession. During the *'slow-time'* of many evenings, he would *entertain* us with his music. He could play *anything! You name it – and he could play it!* We'd just *close our eyes,* and he would *send us home with a favorite song!*

Along our way across Europe, if he came across an accordion that he liked better *(than his),* he would *take* it and leave *his* in its place! He always said he *'liberated'* that accordion! He was *really thrilled* when he came across a *piano!*

'Mo' was also good at *sewing!* While *'holding-up'* in Monschau, before the "Battle of the Bulge," he came across a *sewing-machine,* and a pile of German army *blankets.* It happened to be December and very *cold!* What did he do? He started making *'boot-liners'* out of the blankets! They made a big difference for a lot of us, too! Thank you, *'Mo!'* He was *'quite a guy.'*

26

Night of December 16th . . . Battle of the Bulge

DECEMBER WAS A *very active* month, to say the *least*! On December 1st, we had moved 18 miles from our position in Belgium, to *Monschau,* Germany. We no sooner got there, when the enemy started *'lopping-in' harassing missions.* On the 10th, a Brigadier General from 5th Corps Headquarters visited our position. He took personal notice of the *'Phantom Battalion!'* On the 13th, Battery-C was heavily *shelled* by mortars. Seven men were *injured.* Also on the 13th, we carried on *heavy firing* in support of the 2nd Infantry Division and the 78th Infantry. A-Battery received heavy *mortar* fire, but *no* injuries!

Again, on December 16th, the battalion was heavily *shelled.* The enemy was trying to *'soften us* up' for their last big offensive, to begin later that same night. Also discovered that day were *11 enemy supply parachutes,* including *flares,* all of which we *destroyed.* Nightly enemy *air activity* was increasing.

We were all settled in a little town, *Monschau,* in Germany that we took cover in for about 2 weeks. It was one of the few times that we actually had a real roof over our heads, although the particular house we were in had been '*bombed-out*' and was in *shambles*. Even so, we thought it was *great at the time!*

The war was at a '*stand-still*,' and had been for some time. We had our artillery guns '*dug in place*' all around the town, and occasionally we would fire a '*harassing* mission' just to let the Germans know we were there. Like I say, we were real comfortable there, and so we thought the Colonel had gone *berserk* when, on the night of December 16th, 1944 at about 10 p.m. or so, he issued a '*march-order!*'

'*He's crazy!*' we thought. '*Why move from here? We like it here!*' But move we did. We went about 4 miles, and wound-up on the 1st Army's left flank, in the Ardennes Forest.

We no sooner got there, and barely got our guns in place, when '*all Hell broke loose!*' *And I mean in a big way!* It was the start of the **"Battle of the Bulge,"** the last big German offensive of the war.

It was a clear, moon-lit night. Luckily, we had the '*lay of the land*' in our favor in the forest, *with only 1 road leading in, and out, on the German side.* The enemy, *obviously*, didn't know we were there. Their tanks came sailing towards us on the 1 road leading in. We could hear their loud, '*clanking*' noise long before we could actually see them.

Suddenly, the lead tank appeared, just coming over the top of the hill. I remember Sergeant Zoller ordered his Howitzer to be turned around and pointed at the tank, and fired *point-blank!* This *knocked-out* the *lead* tank. With the road being so narrow, and the thickness of the trees, the following tanks couldn't maneuver around it!

The officer in charge then ordered a '*fire-mission*' on the *end* of the tank column, and *then* on the ones in between! This stopped then in their tracks! If it hadn't been for the *1 road in and out* and the thickness of the forest, we may not have survived this assault!

Almost immediately after this occurrence, in an open space directly to the rear of us, a German plane dropped some paratroopers to try and take us. This was *short-lived!* So, after this, they simply '*skirted*' our position, and passed us by. *Lucky for us!*

Sometime later we passed through our little town of Monschau . . . *There was nothing left of it.* All the troops left there were either *killed* or *captured*. Seeing this, *we didn't think so badly of our Colonel after all!* (We had left there in such a hurry that we had left a large cache of ammo; so now we had returned to get it. It was all still there and quite safe.)

For the next several days, the enemy launched *heavy counter-attacks* on our battalion. On the 20th, we fired *250 rounds* in support of the 196th F.A. Battalion into *Hofen*, Germany. All day, we repelled *heavy* enemy attacks. A few days later, 4 enemy *parachutists* were captured in C-Battery area.

On December 13th, 14th, and 15th, the battalion, in preparation, fired *counter-battery* and *harassing-missions*, to the extent of **400** *rounds per day*, average! An enemy *counter-attack* against the 78th Infantry Division was '*beaten-back*' with the help of our battery.

Now we were introduced to the new '*Pozit*' *fuse*. We couldn't use it if any of our planes were in the air at the time, because, as reported by some captured P.O.W.s, the shells would burst at about *30 feet from the ground*! That was the purpose, to inflict more '*shrapnel*' on the enemy. They reported that the '*shrapnel*' had such force that it would penetrate '*12-inch logs*!'

After the 16th, every morning at dawn, the Germans would shell our position with *heavy* concentrations. Most of this was coming from a *valley*, east of *Imgenbootch*. Finding this out, the next day, before dawn, we laid a *huge* concentration into the valley. This *silenced* the enemy to the extent that they either *left* the area, or were so heavily inflicted that they could *no longer fight*.

Due to the heavy fighting, we were still living on rations (C and K). What I wouldn't have given for some of *Mom's home-cooking* about then! It was as cold as the *arctic* and with *deep* snow in December. We supported the 1st and 9th Infantry Divisions most of the time, occupying several different positions. Eighteen men were *injured* during this month, with *1 case of venereal disease, the only case reported on the continent*! . . . As stated in the official report of the battalion!

It was on the night of December 19th, that the 38th Cavalry Machine-Gun Team, which had been assigned to protect our '*out-post*,' was *withdrawn*, and was *replaced* by a team from A and B-Batteries. *I was one of them*! I was very *un-acquainted* with a *50-caliber machine-gun*! The *carbine* was my '*buddy*.' In teams of 4 men each, we occupied 2 out-posts. Each was placed in a cove of trees. Each of us would take turns '*manning*' the machine-gun, while the other 3 tried to '*catch a few winks*.' Luckily, while I was on duty, there was no enemy action that night. The following night, the other guys took over.

On December 18th, the night before, heavy enemy *tank* attacks in the vicinity of *Hofen* were '*beaten back*' by this battalion. In the secret 'A-and-A Report' of the 186th F.A. Battalion for the month of December reads:

"From December 18th-22nd, the enemy was very active in the area east of Monschau, and north and east of Hofen. Visibility continued to be very poor, but forward observers and listening-posts were often able to report the effectiveness of the well-placed artillery fire of this unit. A number of Infantry attacks against Monschau, and many Infantry and tank attacks against Hofen, were successfully disrupted and beaten-back by the well-placed fire of this battalion and the supported units. Activity rose to a peak on December 22nd, on which day this unit fired 38 missions, expending 1,023 rounds of ammunition!"

(More gun-barrels to be replaced!)

This, evidently, silenced the Germans to almost a '*stand-still.*' For the next (and last) 9 days of December, about the only missions fired were '*harassing-missio*ns' and '*counter-battery.*'

Over **7,000** *rounds of ammo* were fired in **December** of **1944** by our battalion! This was the largest amount to date for us. Although the last of the month was *quiet* in our area, not far to the south, in Ardennes salient, the fighting was *heavy.*

This year, Christmas passed us by: but, my thoughts and prayers were with all my *loved-ones back at home*, as, I'm sure, *theirs* were with *me*. There was no mention of activity on this day in the battalion report. I don't remember if the Chaplain had services on Christmas. If so, they would have been held in the woods amid *heavy snow* and *freezing temperatures*! We did have Sunday services whenever and wherever possible.

In January, though we supported only 4 different outfits, we still expended the monthly average of ammo. We had moved to *Hattlich*, Belgium on the 1st. We were in support of the 9th Infantry, and, on different dates, we supported their 3 artillery battalions. We also supported the V Corps offensive, which was still in progress. The German V-1s ('*Buzz-Bombs*') were still *buzzing* over our positions, quite often at night. On several occasions, enemy fighter-aircraft would fly over our area at a low altitude, possibly on a photographic mission.

The general health of the battalion had been excellent, considering the low *temperatures* and *deep snows*. During December and January, we received *inoculations* for *Typhoid*. We were still in the general area that we were when the '*Bulge*' offensive began. There had been a lot of activity in this area, and there still was. This was the *Monschau* area, which had various military objectives. The 38th Cavalry, which we supported, was credited with *holding the line* against the German *assault*! . . . In the *Ardennes*-part of the *Monschau* area. The German offensive *over-ran* many towns and villages, *killing or capturing everyone in its path*, including *Monschau*.

It was in January that my *Christmas mail* caught up with me. Mom and the girls sent *several* packages of *'goodies'* – *m-m-m-m-m* . . . *good*! I received more letters from Kenny. I assume he received some from me, too, as we kept in touch. Every time I saw one of our fighter-planes, I thought of him.

On February 1st, the battalion moved into position at Hattlich, Belgium with the 9th U.S. Infantry, in support of the V Corps. On the 5th, we moved to Murringen, Belgium . . . then to the vicinity of *Hersched*, Germany. In the missions fired there, most were put on *retreating* enemy troops. The 9th and 78th Divisions performed a *strong* attack on the *Schmidt* and the *Schwammenauel* Dam. Maximum ammo was fired in this action, limited only by the difficulty of *hauling* the ammo over the very *muddy* and almost *impossible* supply route!

After the *capture* of the *all-important* Roer River Dam, the number of missions dropped off sharply. This was even to the point that on February 13th, the whole Battalion didn't fire even *1 round*! This ended an unbroken succession of **113 days** of *consecutive firing*! Up to this date, the weather prevented *'observed missions,'* but from the middle of the month onward, our pilots flew 27 *'observed missions!'*

We were now in support of the 69th Infantry Division. Towns such as *Konzen, Imgenbroish, Eickersched, Rohern,* and *Hammon* were *completely destroyed* by the *'Phantom Battalion,'* our 186th Field Artillery Battalion (F.A. Bn.). Enemy supply lines leading in and out of those towns were crowded with *destroyed enemy vehicles, broken wagons, and dead horses.* Our battalion fired so many rounds, that the affected area was heavily scattered with *shell fragments*, due to the use of the new *'Pozit' fuse*. We *destroyed* 7 *positions* using *rocket projectors*, all with some missions being observed from the air.

On *'counter-battery'* attacks against us, sometimes the wiring would be broken *'here-and-there,'* so I would be one of the men to go repair them, sometimes while *'in-coming'* rounds of enemy *fire* were upon us.

The worst scenario was this happening at *night*, with mud or snow to contend with; but we always made it!

Over **8,000** *rounds* were fired by the battalion in **February** against **304** *targets*! Business was picking up! *'Buzz-bombs'* continued to pass over our area during the month. Battery-C position was bombed by 2 enemy aircraft on February 2nd, where 4 small bombs were dropped, but there were no casualties. It seemed like the Germans were always *'picking on* C-Battery! Forty-five missions were flown by our *'spotter'* planes this month, for a total of over 55 hours flying time. The health of the unit fared well in February.

In March, we started out supporting the 69th Infantry at *Murringen*, Germany . . . moving to *Norrenberg*, Germany on the 7th. On the 8th of the month, again, we moved, this time to *Sehmotheim*. The next day, the 186th went into a *'bivouac'* status. For 3 days we *rested*! *Finally, some rest!* This was the first time we were out of action since *September 10th, 1944*! This ended *6 months* and 1 day of *continuous fighting, moving, fighting, and moving again*; surviving enemy *attacks* from the *air, by their infantry, tanks,* and *artillery*! We had fired some **45,000 rounds** of ammo during this *6-month period!*

After our *'rest-period'* was over, we received a *'march-order'* to proceed eastward toward the *Rhine*! In 3 days, we were firing our first round across the Rhine River! Here we were in support of the 9th Armored Division, 1st Army's *'bridge-head'* over the Rhine!

During **March**, we supported 6 different units in 12 different locations, in a *slow* month of ammo expenditures, with *only* **3,100** *rounds fired*. The health of the outfit remained high. The 5th Corps *dentist* arrived to afford *dental work* to anyone needing it!

One enemy air-craft, an FW190, was *shot down*. The AAA battalion attached to us *shot down* one ME109. On another day, about 12 jet-powered ME262s passed overhead, and *bombed* the *Remagen* Bridge. On March 14th, an unknown number of enemy planes flew over our area *(single-engine fighter planes)*. Four were *damaged* by our attached AAA outfit, but none were *'downed'.*

The weather was still rainy and cold, improving somewhat, but not helping the *morale* much! But the *mail-man* was getting around more often. That really helped! *Thanks, Mom, Fran, Jo, and Edie, too.*

The lines of marching P.O.W.s seemed to be getting longer. They were marching to the rear echelon, where they would be detained in camps. As we traveled from one location to another, we always saw a lot of *wrecked German tanks, artillery guns, trucks, downed aircraft, and dead animals.* The animals are victims of *concussion,* from *shelling* and *shell fragments.* Practically every animal we saw was *dead.*

April of **1945** was *very active.* As the war was coming to an end, the Germans were '*on the run.*' On April 1st, this battalion was attached to the 9th U.S. Armored Division of the 1st Army. The 9th Armored had *circled* south of the Ruhr Valley, and had almost *closed the trap* with the 9th U.S. Army! . . . Which had driven through north of the Ruhr.

According to the battalion report, while in position at *Engar,* Germany, they got word that a group of enemy infantry of some *1,000 strong,* with a number of *tanks,* had begun an attack from the west, trying to break out of the impending '*en-circlement.*' During the night of the 1st and 2nd, they had *captured* the town of *Bonenberg.* This was only about 3 miles from our position. Our artillery fire was placed on this town. One of our '*spotter*' planes observed and immediately adjusted the fire on a number of enemy tanks, forcing them to scatter into the woods.

All day and night, the 186th fired on German infantry and tanks until the town of Bonenberg was *re-taken.* Seven enemy tanks were *destroyed,* and a number of others driven out or range to the north.

From V Corps Headquarters, the 9th Armored Division received orders to attack to the East, moving in 3 columns. Division artillery requested that Battery-A of the 186th be attached to the 73rd Armored Division Field Artillery Battalion. The 73rd Armored ran into *heavy* '*anti-aircraft*' *defensive fire* around Leipzig. In response, our artillery fired a number of accurately placed missions, *knocking-out* 1 battery *of 8, 88-mm guns!* A forward observer with the 16th Armored F.A. Battalion adjusted the firing.

For 2 days in April, the 21st and 22nd, our battalion was attached to the 69th Infantry Division Artillery, and we *fired* **2,282** *rounds* into the town of *Eillenberg,* Germany, *totally destroying it!* Imagine: **2,282** *rounds* in a **48-hour period***! Unbelievable! That's over 47 rounds per hour, continuously for 48 hours! Surely many gun-barrels had to be replaced, although the official report does not mention it.*

This battle was the only '*big action*' of firing for the 186th for the month, as only **3,872** *rounds,* including the 2-day period of 2,282 rounds, were fired.

In April, the 186th Phantom Battalion, for the first time, ran a camp for *Allied P.O.W.s* who were *recovered*. Between the 24th and the 29th, approximately *2400 treatments* were afforded the men in our *first-aid station.* 148 patients were evacuated. There were *18 Americans, 3 Canadians, 74 British, 47 French, 1 Polish, 1 Dutch, and 4 civilians.*

April saw the most activity from the German *air-force.* They seemed to *own* the air! The AAA platoon attached to our outfit said that they expended more ammo this *week* than for any *month* of the war! **35** *missions* were flown over our area. Ten ME109 *planes* escorted 2 regiments *of S.S. Troopers.* Seven of the planes *bombed* an empty field just about *1,000 yards north of our battery!* The other 109s flew low over our area, but did not attack.

On April 11th, we were on '*march-order*' in *daylight!* Another battalion traveling just ahead of us was attacked by 7 ME109s, '*strafing*' and *bombing* the column. Our column was not attacked. God was with us again, as on many occasions.

One other day in April, a regiment of *SS Troopers attacked* our left flank, with added support from a German tank unit at *Paderborn.* Our two battalion observer planes took to the air to direct the firing on the SS troops. This time, 2 enemy tank attacks, of 3 tanks each, were repelled due to the accurate firing of the 186th, as directed by the '*spotter*' pilots.

An enormous amount of credit must be given to our battalion *pilots* for their *good work* all through the *entire* war. One of these was a Lieutenant that I knew personally. He was a '*heck of a nice guy*' from Kansas named Garrett. On one occasion, he ran into heavy '*flak*' while flying close to the outer defensive area of Leipzig, causing *smoke* to come up through the *cockpit*, making him think the plane was on *fire!* Through his evasive action, he was able to make it back to a *safe* landing, though. (*What an experience that must have been!*)

On the 1st of May, we were with the 5th Corps Artillery at Geferees, Germany. On the same day, we were placed at *Hershfield*, to help the 7th F.A. Battalion. Two days later, we were ordered to go support a battalion of the 38th Infantry Regiment of the 2nd U.S. Infantry Division. This was on May 5th, and on the same day, we moved to Folmava, Czechoslovakia in direct support of the 2nd Division. The next day we were at Paschnitz, Czechoslovakia, and Domazlice. During April and

May, we definitely had the enemy *on the run*. They were '*giving their all*,' in a '*last ditch*' effort.

On May 7th, 1945, President Harry Truman announced to the world that the **8th of May** would be proclaimed **V-E Day** . . . *Victory in Europe Day*! This took 11 months and 2 days to accomplish.

The *last round fired* by my battalion was on May 4th, 1945. Total rounds fired for **May** were only **86!** Although the war was officially over on May 8th, '*mop-up*' operations continued for some time. Our immediate outfit was assigned to *finding* and '*rounding up*' *stray* German *soldiers, and even some whole German units*! At this point, they were ready to surrender!

27

Could it have been Hitler?

I DON'T RECALL the *exact* location, but it was somewhere in southern Germany, just a few days before the end of the war. We approached a small airport, one *so* small we thought it might have been a *private* one.

The rumor was out that *Hitler* was *on the run, trying to escape* to another country. *This rumor fueled our imagination.* Suddenly, we heard the roar of an airplane engine, and a German Luftwaffe plane came streaking down the runway!

There was a tall, wire fence between us and the field and plane. We, some 6 or 7 of us, began *firing* our carbines at the plane!

I know the other guys were all thinking the same thing: *'What if that was Hitler in that plane?'*

None of our shots hit their target, as the plane *lifted-off* and disappeared.

A few days later, we got the news that the war was officially *over*!

28

Snipers in Pilsen

V ICTORY IN EUROPE finally came in May of 1945. Needless to say, everyone was *overjoyed!* Emotions were running *high*. We '*hooped*' and '*hollared*' and threw our *helmets into the sky! Glory be! I t was over!*

A day or two after the war in Europe had officially ended, we had just arrived in Czechoslovakia. It didn't take long for word to get around that in Pilsen, some 50 miles away, there happened to be a *brewery*! *Boy, did that sound good!* We'd been almost a *year* without beer! But *how* could I get there? It was too far to walk.

Luckily, I just happened to be near the 1st Sergeant's post when he got a call from headquarters. Each battery was to send 1 vehicle, with 6 volunteers *(24 in all)*, into the city of Pilsen to help '*clean-out*' some snipers still '*holding-out*' there! . . . *What luck!* . . . *I immediately volunteered! I could taste the beer already!*

In a matter of hours, we pulled into town. We did encounter a *few* snipers, but with a convoy of *4 vehicles and 24 armed men*, we soon *discouraged* them. Now we were free to *explore* for a while.

I was just wondering, "*Where in the 'heck' is that brewery!?*" . . . when, soon, I saw a couple other G.I.s *staggering* down the street! They pointed the way there.

It was an impressive looking building, the type you would imagine being a brewery. As we entered the building (myself and 5 other guys from my outfit), we could hear a lot of *talking* and *laughter*!

A staircase led to the basement where there were several **huge** *beer vats*! They actually *touched the ceiling*! Each had a *spicket* attached, but since we had left our camp-site in a hurry, we never thought of putting on our *canteen* belts! So, what did we drink out of? . . . Problem solved – *our helmets*!

We each took our helmet off, and inspected them all to see which had the *cleanest. (After all, they had been used for so many other things, for so long!)* I imagine they held at least a *gallon*. After picking one, 2 or 3 at a time would share it. The beer was *ice-cold* and *so good* that we all '*gulped*' it down in *record time*! After no beer for a *full year*, what could you *expect*!? . . . Some time passed, and we all got our fill. *Boy, was that good!* But soon it was time to go. (*By the way, it was here in Pilsen, Czechoslovakia that the light-colored, 'pilsner' beer so popular in the U.S. was invented!*) Good thing the war was *over*, because we were in *no shape to do much about it!*

29

Infection in Domazlice

WE WERE HOUSED in a former German army barracks building in *Domazlice,* Czechoslovakia, which was *quite large* and *'roomy,'* with *'double-deck' bunks.* Mine was on the top. One night, unknowingly, I was *bitten by a spider.* The next morning, I noticed it, but didn't give it much thought. By evening, a *red streak was above my elbow.*

I showed it to the *'medic,'* and he said, *"If it reaches your arm-pit, it could be fatal!"*

He had me take several *aspirins every few hours.* He had a small, portable, Coleman gas-heater on which he heated some *water.* This we poured in my helmet, because it was deeper than anything else we had available. He told me to *soak* my elbow and arm in *hot water* for *20-minutes at a time, at 20-minute intervals.*

He and I stayed up *all night* doing this routine! He *heated* the water and *fed* me *aspirins* throughout the night . . . *and it worked!* By morning, the streak had *receded* to the *middle* of my arm; and, finally, during the day, it *disappeared.* I thought it was really considerate of him to help me all night long. *Thanks pal!* How many other people do you think would have done that?

30

Domazlice

DOMAZLICE, CZECHO-SLOVAKIA WAS a small, but clean and neat, little town, considering that the German Army had occupied it for 6 or 7 years. There was a small, 1-chair *barber-shop* on the main street.

Although, as I mentioned earlier, we had a barber in the outfit, I thought I'd stop in. *And I was so glad that I did.*

To my surprise, the barber spoke *perfect English*! I remarked on that fact, and so he said that he was actually *an **American**! . . . And from **Chicago**!*

"What in the world are you doing over here!?" I asked.

He explained that some years back, he decided to travel through Europe, and when he came across Domazlice, he immediately '*took*' to the town, especially when he found out how far the American dollar went! He claimed he had only about $500. 00 when he '*hit*' town. He went on to say that he seemed to be '*living like a king,*' so he stayed. When the German army came, he was *stuck.*

He said that he had barbered many German soldiers, but only a *few* offered to *pay.* It didn't matter, though. He felt lucky just to be *alive*!

As he trimmed away at my hair, he asked where I was from. "*Quincy, Illinois.*" I replied. "*Quincy!*" he said loudly, "*Heck, I used to go down there to go duck hunting when I lived in Chicago!*" What a small world it was, we both agreed! I finally knew he was telling the truth because he named some places, such as some of the islands where he had hunted. When he mentioned *Clat Adams store*, I knew that he had really been in Quincy. (*Clat Adams' store* was located at *the foot of Hampshire Street*, right on the *river-front*, and in the days of the *'river-boats,'* it was practically a *'trading-post.'*)

Stopping in at his shop made me feel a little closer to home.

On another occasion, four of us went *'bumming around'* Domazlice, and found a *photographer's studio.* As someone suggested, *'Let's all send a photo home,'* we all went in.

It was a *well-equipped* shop. You could tell he was a *'pro.'* He motioned for us to have a seat. Finally, we made him understand what we had in mind.

He motioned for one of us to come forward and sit on a certain *stool* . . . Soon another, then another . . . and finally I said, "*Hey, how about me?*" He smiled, and in his twisted English said that he had *already* taken mine! It seems that as I was sitting there *'day-dreaming,'* he had snapped my picture!

The next day, the developing was done, and we were all satisfied with his work. Quickly, we sent the copies home to our *'folks!'*

31

Ken in Nuremberg

I FORGET THE exact date, but the war was over and I was stationed in Domazlice, Czechoslovakia. Just like back in Camp Kilmer, Fort Dix, New Jersey, I just happened to be in the 1st Sergeants office when he got word that one of the guys' parents had *died*. He was given permission to return home to the U.S. In order to do so, he had to be *transported* to *Nuremberg*, Germany, some 75 to 100 miles away. I overheard the 1st Sergeant say that a *'non-commissioned' officer* had to *go along*. Instantly I said, "*Hey, Sarge, how about me? My brother is in Nuremberg.*" He said, "*No, not again!*" . . . With a smile on his face!

Ken was in the 8th Air Force, and he was stationed in Nuremberg, Germany. This I knew through our correspondence. So, in a matter of hours, the jeep driver, Charlie, and I were on our way.

It was in July, and the weather was nice. I remember arriving at the *'air-base'* right at *meal-time*, just like when I *'popped-in'* on Ken in Ft. Dix! After seeing that Charlie got *'registered-in'* properly to catch his flight home, he, Bob and I were told where the *'mess-hall'* was.

Once we got there, I inquired whether anyone knew where Kenny might be. Someone *pointed out* where he was sitting; and again, *just like in Ft. Dix, I came up behind him*; and as *I 'strattled' the seat on the* *bench, I tapped him on the shoulder, and like before, I said, "**Hey, buddy, pass the salt.**"*

As he turned his head, I was standing there smiling. He about *jumped out of his shoes! Again, he just couldn't believe it!* All his buddies sitting *close-by laughed* and were again *glad* for us.

We enjoyed our meal together and visited. We sure had fun talking about the letters we were getting from home, and about the family. I stayed *over-night* with Ken, and I sure enjoyed that. Ken really *'got a bang out of it'* when I told him about my 1st Sergeant *(his comical response)!* *"Maybe I'll meet him,"* he said, with a little *smile* of his own. *"I can get a pass, and go back with you."* he said. *"That would be great!"* I replied. So, we went back to my base together.

The trip back was in the dark. Now, all military vehicles have just *'half-headlights,'* as the *top-half* is *blackened-out,* to help prevent being seen at night. The jeep driver and I were very well *accustomed* to *night-driving,* as the artillery always traveled after dark, *but Ken was not!* The road was *bumpy* and *twisting,* and sitting in the back-seat, Ken and I *felt it all!* Not being used to this sort of thing, when we got to my barracks, he said, *"Wow! What a ride!"* He liked it so much that he *'hitch-hiked'* back to his base the next day!

He did get to meet my 1st Sergeant, though; *after all, the 'Sarge'* was responsible for our two *surprise meetings!* At that point, I said, *"I'll see you in Japan!"* as we were both alerted to *go there in August.*

Instead, President Harry Truman dropped the atomic bomb on Japan *(2 of them),* thus ending the war over there. At this we were all *'thrilled to high-heaven,'* knowing that now, we would soon be going home, and that the *whole* war was over.

Some two-months later, *we were homeward bound.*

Rough ride!

32

The Fast Buck

THE NIGHT I *'stayed-over'* with Ken in Nuremberg, he wanted to hear of some of my *experiences* along the way. I mentioned the time that we stopped by an old farm-house that had been *'bombed-out,'* and all over the front yard were all kinds of German *currency*! I thought that it was no longer any good, but, just for *souvenirs*, I picked up 2 *1000 Mark notes*, which I had with me. I showed them to Ken and his buddies, and Ken was *excited*! *"These are worth $100. a-piece!"* he said. *"Where?"* I asked. He said that he could *cash them in* for American money at *his base*.

I gave him *one* of the notes to *cash-in* for me, and told him to mail me the money, which he later did. I still have the other. *I still think of all that money laying on the ground there in that yard, and of how I only picked-up 2! Oh, well! You win some; you lose some!*

33

V-E Day

VICTORY IN EUROPE came in May of 1945, and it generated *celebrations all over the world!* I remember that in our '*outfit,* we went *crazy!* We *yelled* and *hollered!* And went around *hitting each-other playfu lly!* . . . Throwing our *helmets* in the air, as if to say, *"We won't need these anymore!"* A keg of Pilsner would have come in handy!

Thoughts of home came automatically. Right then, a *cell-phone* would have been worth *$1,000.* ! I wish I could have been back home at the time, to celebrate with all the family! They wrote, though, and said that *all* of Quincy was *uptown* on Maine Street, *dancing in the street!* . . . *Strangers grabbing one-another, hugging* and *kissing* in *celebration!* I suppose it was the same everywhere.

This was a day for everyone to celebrate, cherish, and remember forever.

In Europe, Hitler made his *last attempt* to win the war on December 16th, 1943, as I said before. His massive '*build-up*' of troops and equipment was *assembled* on a front some *75 miles long.* What was left of the German '*air-force*' was included. He used the dead of winter, which was very cold and snowy, to launch the surprise attack. *And he came close to winning!*

Had he had more men and equipment in the area, he may have won. It was very close. Hitler knew it was his last chance, and the stakes were *'all or nothing.'* His army inflicted *heavy casualties* on the *'allied'* armies, but with our determination, and God on our side, this battle was the last of the *'Big War!'*

As I said, when the news reached our unit, we were *ecstatic!* . . . *thrilled to no end!* We *yelled* and *shouted* and celebrated! And, then, we wondered, *"When do we go home?"* Our next, *immediate*, destination was *Domazlice, which you've heard about*, where we made use of the large, German barracks buildings. We were all anxious to get home, but soon the word came to get ready to go to *Japan! One war wasn't enough!* This dampened our spirits; but if it was to be, so be it.

Before we realized it, August was upon us. We were supposed to *'ship-out'* come September. But, in **August**, President Harry Truman decided to drop the *atomic bomb* on *2* sites in Japan, which ended the war there almost instantly, with the Japanese surrendering. *What a relief! Now we would be heading home!*

34

The Trip Back Home

AS I'VE SAID, I was, of course, *jubilant* at the war's official *ending*. Now I would be *heading home – but when?* We had no idea. But knowing that it was going to happen was something to look forward to.

The next 5 months, from May to October, seemed to *never pass!* *Letter-writing* home was at a *furious* pace. The folks were all *anxious* to know all the particulars of our trip home.

In September, we started getting *physicals*, and *shots*, and *briefing* on our *G.I. Bill of Rights* after *discharge*. "**Discharge**," what a *beautiful sounding word! Oh, to be a civilian again!* Time did pass, and then came October. On about the 18th, we boarded-ship and were on our way.

The trip *home* was *so much different* than the trip *over*, when we were just *heading into war*, and *being hunted by German subs and planes!* This time it was *relaxing*. We spent many hours *just standing* on *deck-side*, *day-dreaming* about being *back at home, with this terrible war behind us*. We were all *relieved* and *anxious* to see our *loved-ones* again, after some 3 years.

The trip home was much shorter than the one going over, too, just **5** days, I recall. In the early morning of the last day, the **New York**

City skyline and, soon thereafter, the *faint figure* of the **Statue of Liberty** appeared on the horizon. *What a sight to behold!*

After arriving at New York City, I was put through the *"military process,"* turning in all of my *military belongings* except the *uniform* on my back and my '*dog-tags!*' After spending a night at a military base, I was *turned loose* and told to catch '*such-and-such*' train to **Chicago.**

Upon arriving in Chicago, to Fort Sheridan I went. There I was '*mustered out,*' given a train ticket home and **$300**. '*mustering out pay!*' I felt *rich*! I received another *physical* and *counseling*! I remember the counselor trying to sell me on the idea of *joining the Army reserves* upon returning home, the sales-pitch being: '*You receive $10. per month for attending only 1 meeting per month.*' That was more than a *third* of my usual *monthly* pay! That sounded good, but not for me. My reply: *"No, thanks. Three years is enough for me. I think I've done my duty."*

This was one of the easiest decisions of my life. One war was enough for me. This was in 1945, and just 5 years later, in 1950, the Korean War began. *The local reserves outfit was on its way . . .*

SECRET
HEADQUARTERS 1ST U.S. INFANTRY DIVISION ARTILLERY
APO #1, U.S. ARMY

2 July 1944

MEMO:

TO : All Bns and Atchd Units.

It is with great pride and pleasure that I send you the following letter. The support mentioned was rendered by the 5th, 7th, 33rd and 186th FA Bns. and unquestionably was of great effect and value.

Comment of this nature from a first class fighting division such as the British 7th Armored Division is specially welcome.

"TO: Commanding General, 1st United States Infantry Division Artillery.

During the pase few weeks of fighting we have formed a tremendous respect and admiration for the Artillery of the United States 1st Infantry Division.

We shall remember particularly your prompt and effective support whilst 7th Armoured Division held Tracy-Bocage against heaty attacks, when the accuracy and weight of the artillery fire caused great losses to our mutual enemy.

The efficiency of the observation officers and the helpful cooperation of the liaison officers we have met could not have been bettered.

The Artillery of the 7th Armoured Division wishes you the best of luck in the future, and looks forward to fighting side by side with you again on our way to Victory."

(Signed) R. Mews
CRA, 7th Armoured Division

/s/Clift Andrus
/t/CLIFT ANDRUS
Brig. Gen. USA.
Arty. Commander.

Reproduced Hq. 186th FA Bn. 5/7 /44 & 5/8/44 RES

HEADQUARTERS 1ST U.S. INFANTRY DIVISION ARTILLERY
APO #1, U.S. ARMY

19 July 1944

SUBJECT: Commendation.

TO   : Commanding General, V Corps Artillery,
          APO #305. (Thru channels).

1. Upon the conclusion of our recent period of service with V
Corps, I desire to express appreciation of the 186th Field Artillery
Battalion.

2. This battalion was attached to 1st Division Artillery upon its
landing and worked with us until our relief from V Corps. Its speed and
accuracy in firing were of prime importance upon several critical occasions.
Its disciplinary and administrative standards were equally as high as those
of gunnery.

3. The entire 1st Division Artillery has deserved respect and admiration for the 186th Field Artillery Battalion and earnestly hopes that the for-
tunes of war may again enable us to welcome it back as a member of our battle
team.

/s/ Clift Andrus
/t/ CLIFT ANDRUS
Brig. Gen., USA
Arty. Commander

I certify this to be a true copy:

W G BATTON
Captain, FA

SOURCES

ALL TECHNICAL INFOR-MATION, dates and paths of military movement, and military statistics contained in this book were taken from the official: **A/A ('After Action') Report** for our **186ᵗʰ Field Artillery Battalion** of the **United States Army**, which is now '*de-classified*' and available to the public at the:

National Archives
Washington, D.C.